Chapter 1 - Introduction

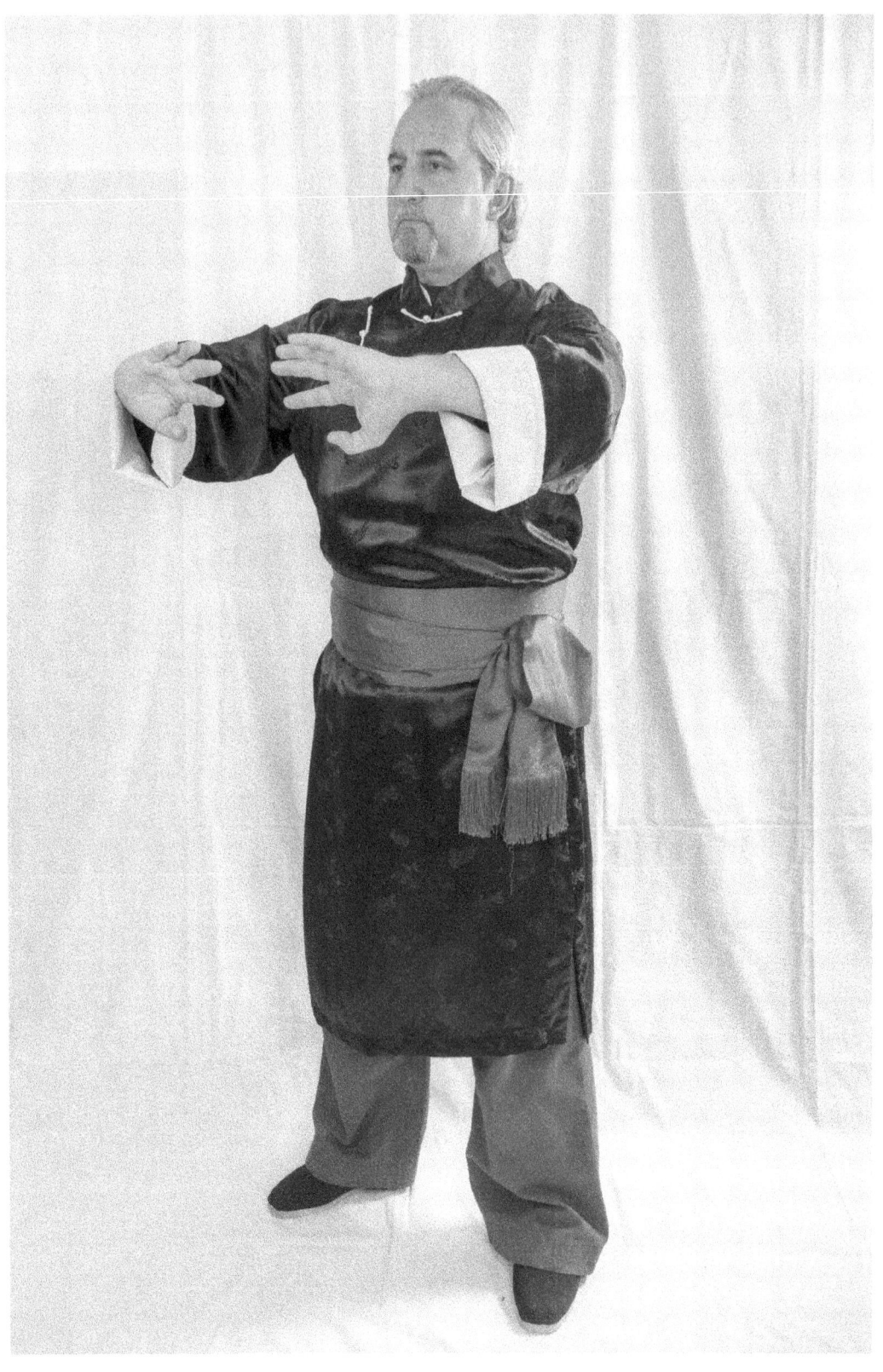

Pai Lum Tao's INTERNAL HAND

By:

Grandmaster Glenn C. Wilson (2012)

Copyright © 2012 by WDWS Publications

All rights reserved. This book or any portion thereof may not be reproduced or used in any manner whatsoever without the express written permission of the publisher.

Printed in the United States of America

First Printing, 2012

ISBN 978-0-9858411-0-2

WDWS Publications

955 W. Lancaster Rd, Suite #1

Orlando, FL 32809

USA

www.pailum.org

Disclaimer

Please note that the author and publisher of this book are NOT RESPONSIBLE in any manner whatsoever for any injury that may result from practicing the techniques and/or following the instruction given within. Since the physical activities described herein may be too strenuous in nature for some readers to engage in safely, it is essential that a physician be consulted prior to training.

Preface

The wisdom of the teacher that is passed down from generation to generation becomes priceless to the grateful student. The student aspires to master 'the way'. Society benefits from the lessons taught and as a culture we spread and share the many benefits of an ancient and at time spiritual message. We learn from the internal teachings of 'The way of the white dragon' to seek peace always. Yet if need be, the Pai Lum Tao students is equipped with the 'Grand Ultimate Fist'.

Within the four establish disciplines of the revered Pai Lum Tao system of martial arts which is regarded as a 'way of life' by many. One has the opportunity to study and practice the 'Internal hand of the White Dragon'. The study of Pai Yung Tai Chi, Quan Yen Chi Kung and Chin Kon Pai meditation are available to the aspiring student who chooses the path of the White Dragon way of life.

Within the Internal Hand training an emphasis is put on internal as well as external health, mental strength, balance of life as well as an ancient system of self defense. A practitioner learns the values of balancing ones mind, body and spirit in a natural manner. The mind is expanded through harmonious movements while the body is stretched and strengthened through non evasive well balanced patterns and movements.

Mental health, depleted stress and anxiety, physical power and a heightened sense of inner peace are at the center of the training. This is a true gift to ones self that benefits everyone that is associated with the practitioner. Pai Lum Tao's internal hand training is a true gift to all that practice the teachings and share their good energy with all.

Table of Contents

Table of Contents

Chapter 1 - Introduction	10
Chapter 2 - Philosophy	26
Chapter 3 - Quan Nien Chi Kung	36
Chapter 4 - Pai Yung Tai Chi	102
Chapter 5 - Virtues of the Nine Creatures and Five Elements	138
Chapter 6 - Massage	166
Chapter 7 - Health and Happiness	178
Chapter 8 - Blocks	186
Chapter 9 - Punches	192
Chapter 10 - Stances	198

Acknowledgements

I find that when authoring any type of writing that will be a part of one's martial arts style and the history of that style, it is only accomplished with the great efforts of many people. There is no price that you can put on the passion and hard work that others offer so freely and generously. Such efforts are a testimony to the strength and resolve of our Pai Lum Tao family of martial arts. I thank God and our family every day for being given such a gift. The internal knowledge that Dr. Daniel K. Pai and Simo Denise Vigi passed on to us is priceless.

I would like to acknowledge the following for their tremendous contributions to this labor of love – Pai Lum Tao's Internal Hand.

Hilda G. Wilson – Research and unwavering support

Bryan Naegele – technical expertise, support and photography

Dr. Robert Murphy – Research and outstanding support

Caroline Chen Whately – Research and outstanding support

Joe McGuire RN– research

Conrad Blasko – research

All my students who modeled for the photos

White Dragon Warrior Society members – support

I would like to give a special thank you to my direct teacher, 'the late' Great Grandmaster Dr. Daniel Kalimaahaae 'Kane' Pai for the many years of guidance, teachings, patients, support and fatherly love that he gave me. Through my young years as an adolescent Sifu to my years as an experienced master, he was there for me. He led me with his own unique way of doing things. Dr. Pai will always be remembered as one of the foremost teachers of our times and a martial artist who is recognized as a true legend in his own time.

Thank you to Simo Denise Vigi. She was the love of Dr. Pai's life and his soul mate. They are together now in the after life performing their Tai Chi Chuan and Chi Kung. Simo Denise was the premier internal stylist in Pai Lum Tao and we miss her graceful movements and her willingness to share her knowledge with all of us.

Dedication

I would like to dedicate this book to the following:

My family, for their never ending support and patience during all my Martial Arts endeavors. As any prosperous Martial Arts teacher will tell you, it takes a lot of support from those closest to you to be successful.

With honor to my Martial Arts family, Gong Yuen Chuan Fa – Pai Pao Lung Gar. I am blessed as a leader/father of my own family of Pai Lum Tao martial arts. I am truly honored to have such wonderful and giving people to train with and share our knowledge together. They are always here for me and I strive to give the same.

I will always show the greatest admiration and respect to my teacher, (the late) Great Grandmaster – Dr. Daniel Kalimaahaae Pai. It has been years since his passing and journey to our Lord. His teachings and guidance I will forever hold close to my heart. His teachings will endure for centuries to come.

I give special dedication to the late Simo Denise Vigi. She was an inspiration to all she knew. She lead a spiritual life that most can only dream of and few can come close to in their lives. Her knowledge and skill of the internal arts was a sight to behold and treasured. My family was blessed to be with her to her last day and her journey to pure peace.

Chapter 1 - Introduction
Order of Rank and Virtue

Rank	Virtue
Black IX	Humility
Black VIII	Eminent
Black VII	Superlative
Black VI	Authority
Black V	Nobility
Black IV	Mastery
Black III	Creativity
Black II	Leadership
Black I	Enlightenment
Brown 1	Proficiency
Brown 2	Diligence
Green	Persistence
Blue	Inspiration
Purple	Animation
Orange	Exhilaration
Yellow	Stimulation
White	Birth

Chapter 1

Introduction

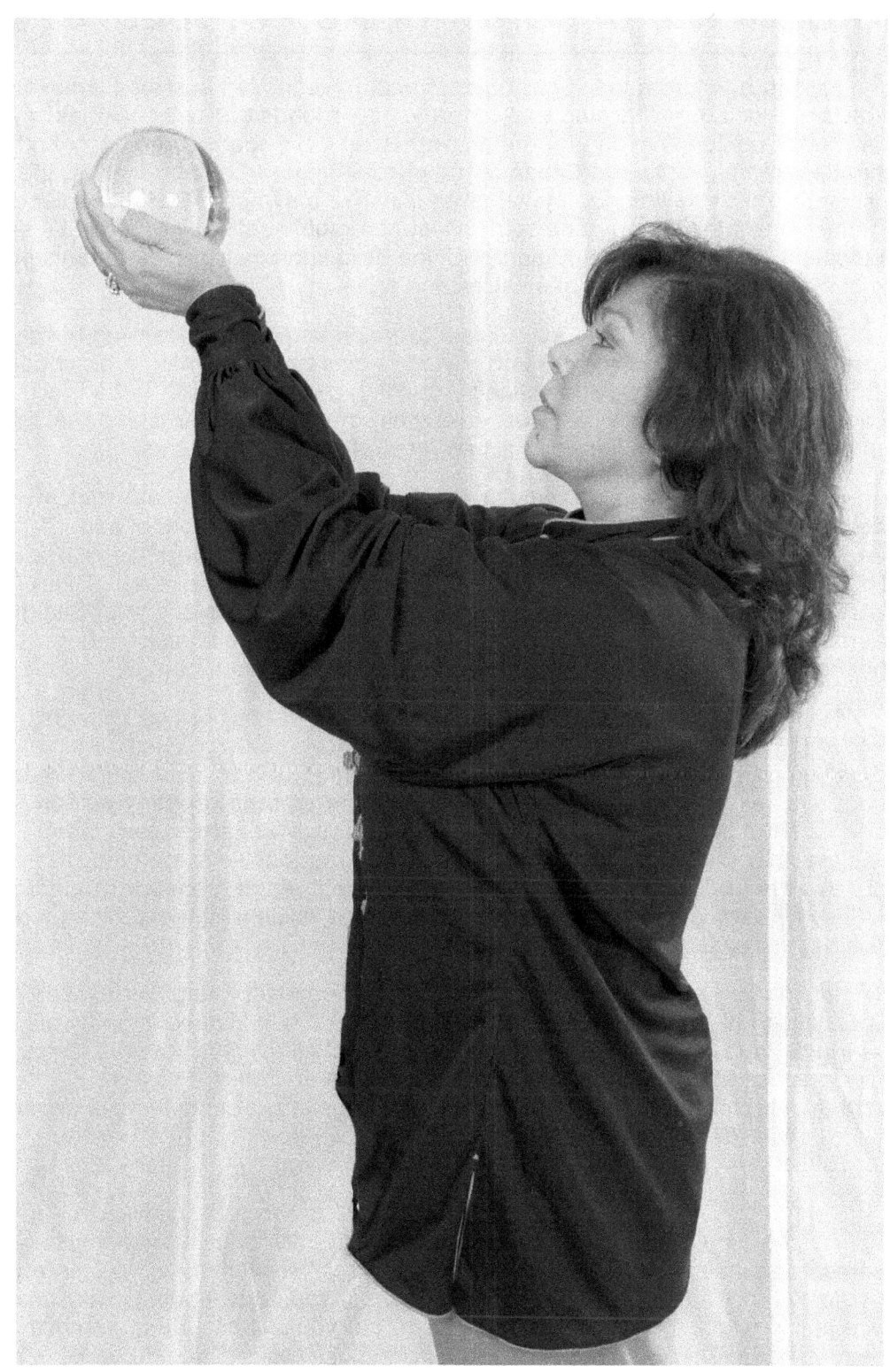

Benefits of Tai Chi Chuan Practice

For those who are looking for better health, reduction in stress, innovative mental conditioning, recharging their energy, new friends and relationships and overall better perspective on life, the answer is Tai Chi Chuan. Often described as 'meditation in motion' Tai Chi Chuan is truly the ultimate in balancing ones life. The smooth, fluid prearranged movements play like a symphony of movement that tames one's mind, body and spirit. Most commonly believed to have it's early development in the Cheng Du region of China, it is known also to be an ancient form of self defense for those of all sizes and ages.

The practice of Tai Chi Chuan is set in a non competitive learning format. It is truly an art, not a sport! Through rhythmic exercise movement a practitioner find their own place in time and space by building their own worth in their art. The practice of the movements, postures, stretches, breathing patterns and mental focus the student will surely rise to a new level of contentment.

There are patterns and exercises that will concentrate on nature elements as well as the virtues of various animals. We learn as humans to feel and appreciate what we have all around us on a daily basis. We can get so wound up in our daily work habits that we forget to stop and 'smell the roses'. Then the stress of our chosen habits and life styles catch up with us and poor health consumes us. Tai Chi Chuan provides an alternative life style choice to the mundane life of poor physical health and destructive mental thoughts.

Many Tai Chi Chuan practitioners have spoken of the positive benefits of recovering following surgery. The non evasive movements coupled with harmonious rhythm of motion and balanced breathing, the body begins to react in a positive self healing manner. It is well documented that for many persons recovering from surgery that have experienced a much easier recovery time. They claim that their body feels the soft rhythmic motions as something that is a natural stimulus to their healing process. In recent years the western medical societies have accepted and are now promoting this ancient Chinese art as a plus for their patients during recovery.

Practitioners have raved and claimed to be in better health with life's health challenges such as cardio functions, respiratory challenges, high blood pressure, diabetes, arthritis, chronic pain and the digestive system. Yes, through regular practice of this most magnificent expression of stance – posture – execution of technique and breathing patterns thousands of people have sworn that they have felt their ailments get better and they now maintain a better quality of life.

Tai Chi Chuan can be practiced anywhere. One can practice their routines in a park, backyard, living room, bedroom, office or bathroom. Curtail your movements to match your environment. When stress sneaks up on you, escape into your own private zone of comfort and healing. Your surroundings will surely dictate much of what you are able to perform, but you will be able to practice some form of Tai Chi Chuan. Even if you are in your auto driving and your stressful day is catching up with you, practice the ancient forms of breathing to reduce and possibly remove your stress. It is after all, your space, your mind-body and your gift to yourself.

It is important to set aside time for you and your health - both mental and physical. Recharge your battery; yes get more energy through the soft rhythmic motions of Tai Chi Chuan. We all speak of exercising on a regular basis; there is no more perfect balance of physical exercise and mental calmness. Consider it your personal 'time out' time, a mini vacation of peace and caring for your needs. All one needs to do is decide to 'do it', then the process begins. With very little preparation and planning you can transfer your state of mind to a new level of calmness and ultimately a place of utmost peace.

How does one know when they need to practice their Tai Chi Chuan? With regular practice the senses are sharpened and a greater self awareness is developed. We get to know ourselves through 'inner searching' and a greater understanding of what our own needs and desires may hold. A state of 'self awareness' is so very important for all people. Before we can help others around us, we must first understand and help ourselves. This is a great benefit of regular practice and becomes our own therapeutic instrument.

With regular practice one learns to 'let go of what is not desired or needed'. During the travel or process of building this new 'self discovery' one learns to pace themselves and know when urgency is required and when it is not. With every breathe inhaled and exhaled during practice we enhance our mental and physical health which in turn balances our emotional state much like the steadiness of 'yin and yang'.

With much input from Tai Chi Chuan organizations, individuals who have studied and benefited from regular practice and comprehensive studies in the medical and psychological fields, we know that this ancient art form has many benefits and rewards. For example such behaviors as mood swings, anxiety, depression, anger, fatigue are lessened and in many cases eliminated.

Several studies performed worldwide have concluded that adults as well as children have shown a lower level of stress and anxiety after regular practice. Adults showed changes in their respiratory and cardiovascular systems as well as electroencephalographic and lower stress hormone levels. Adults have shown signs of better decision making and longer attention and retention in the work place.

Children have become calmer and have even displayed lower levels of emotional stress, hyperactivity, frustration and even cortisol levels. With very little or no side effects children become in more control of their own behavior and choose a calmer and more positive approach to challenges. Mental and emotional stress or minimized and in with continued practice a child may stabilize to a calmer life style. This is a positive course for them, family members and friends. All aspects of their lives are affected with a minimal yet regular schedule of Tai Chi Chuan practice.

It has become clear to the western world that the benefits of Tai Chi Chuan practice that the eastern world has known for centuries are priceless. What the Chinese have coined as the 'mind – body – spirit' medicine has now impacted the world. The interaction that takes place during practice of the brain and body trigger a positive thought and physical reaction. Ones mental, emotional and social behavior are enhanced and helped to follow a more positive path. We learn to establish our own self care and then we happily share that energy with others.

Most people choose to practice Tai Chi Chuan for its obvious mental and physical health benefits. It is very important to remember that this ancient Chinese art is also revered Martial Arts. Thus it maintains and propagates a self defense that can enrich everyone's lifestyle. The smooth, gentle, non aggressive movements are based in self defense philosophies. The animals and elements that are mastered through diligent and prolonged practice are precious to the practitioner. The 'Grand Ultimate Fist' name is believed to describe the mere fact that it can be practiced throughout one's life. By applying the concepts of 'marriage of motion' one can feel the self defense benefits almost immediately. It is very important to remember that all of the Pai Lum Tao disciplines of training, ultimate self defense are at the very core of the teaching.

Great Grandmaster Dr. Daniel Kalimaahaae Pai
Orlando, FL - 1992

Great Grandmaster
Dr. Daniel Kalimaahaae 'Kane' Pai

Great Grandmaster- Pai Lum Tao Martial Arts
10th Level Pai Te Lung Chuan Kung Fu
Master Level - Bok Leen Pai Kenpo
Master Level – Hawaiian Kempo
5th Level Okinawan Kempo
5th Level Aikido
5th Level Jiu Jitsu
Master Level – Pai Yung Tai Chi
Master Level – Quan Nien Chi Kung

Chapter 1 - Introduction

Daniel Kane Pai was born April 4, 1930 in Kameulai Hawaii. He lived the last seventeen years of his life in Florida and passed away in 1993 in the Dominican Republic. Per his request he was laid to rest in his beloved Hawaii. During his sixty-three year journey on earth he built a martial arts legacy throughout North America leaving only five heads of family, a few Sigung's and several Sifu's to carry on the teachings of the 'Way of the White Dragon'. A truly controversial figure, Daniel Kane Pai did it his way, from the tough streets of Hawaii to forming the largest Kung Fu system in North America during the 60's and 70's. There was no doubt of his command of Pai Lum Tao Martial Arts. He taught a rough/tough type of training, for which the Hawaiian Islands are well known. A young Daniel began training with family members in Hawaii in the disciplines of Kung Fu, Kenpo and Judo-Jujitsu. He would master 'the Pai family' martial arts which contained mainly elements of Dragon and Crane. After the mastery of Dragon and Crane, the Tiger, Leopard and Snake were introduced to the young practitioner.

His life reflected many changes. He was a teacher of martial arts, a graduate of the Chicago Medical College "Ph.D.", a bodyguard, stunt coordinator, and cowboy at the Parker Ranch, Philosopher, biker and decorated Korean War Veteran. In the seventies, Dr. Pai formed the U.S. White Dragon Martial Arts Society in hopes of standardizing his vast knowledge of martial arts. The students of the sixties and seventies who weathered Pai's rigorous and at times brutal training became known as the "Old School" lineage. Dr. Pai's American team was awarded the Superb Achievement Merit at the Kuoshu event in Taipei in 1976. In 1980 Dr. Pai served as director at the 3rd World Chinese Kuoshu Tournament in Hawaii. During Dr. Pai's visit to Taipei in 1983 he was appointed the United States Vice President of the Worldwide Promotion Association 'Executive Board' of the Kuoshu Federation of the Republic of China. As President of the United States Chinese Kuoshu Federation in 1989 he organized the much-talked about World Chinese Kuoshu tournament in Las Vegas, Nevada.

In 1990 Dr. Pai and disciple Glenn Wilson began work on forming a structured organization to unite the different factions of Pai Lum Tao martial arts, to standardize the curriculum and to legitimize rank. Today this organization is the 'White Dragon Warrior Society'. The Society is 'chaired' by Grand Master Glenn C. Wilson and is dedicated to keeping the dreams of Great Grand Master Daniel Kane Pai alive. Dr. Pai was a true pioneer of Martial Arts in America, a true-life innovator of the modern arts and one of the rare legends in his own time!

Chapter 1 - Introduction

Grandmaster Glenn C. Wilson

'Pai Pao Lung Huit'
'Name given by Great Grandmaster Daniel Kalimaahaae Pai'
5 Times World Champion
8 Times U.S. National Champion
Inducted into 6 Hall of Fames
1984 to 1989 Coach on U.S. National Kung Fu Team
CEO - White Dragon Warrior Society
President - Glenn Wilson's Martial Arts Academies International
Head Coach - Wilson's "Pai Lum Tao" Warriors Team USA
Published author
Film Fight Choreographer
Professor: Gong Yuen Chuan Fa Family

Masters Certifications in:
Pai Te Lung Chuan Kung Fu
Bok Leen Pai Kenpo
Pai Yung Tai Chi Chuan
Quan Nien Chi Kung
Shaolin Chuan Fa / Moi Fah Kung Fu

Proud member of:
Gong Yuen Chuan Fa Federation
White Dragon Warrior Society, Inc.
World Kuoshu Federation
United States Chinese Kuoshu Federation
Pai Lum White Dragon / White Lotus Society
World Head of Family Sokeship Council
Martial Arts Collective Society
Pan China Confederation Martial Arts – Beijing, China
International Chinese Kempo Karate Federation

Grandmaster Wilson is a senior disciple of the late Great Grandmaster Dr. Daniel Kane Pai and was chosen by Dr. Pai to head up The White Dragon Warrior Society and carry on the Pai Lum Tao torch of learning. Glenn now dedicates his martial arts life to keeping the dreams of Daniel Kane Pai alive and educating the world to this most fascinating style.

Grandmaster Wilson has had a truly illustrious career. As a competitor in the seventies he was a member of the U.S. Team and won five world titles and eight U.S. National titles. In the eighties he served for four years as a coach on the U.S. Team. Grandmaster Wilson has appeared in virtually every major Martial Arts magazine and has been voted into 6 Martial Arts Hall of Fames. His book "Pai Lum Tao - Way of the White Dragon" was published by Unique Publications and is the first book ever published on the Pai Lum Tao system

As a personal protection specialist he has secured the safety of such celebrities as Michael Jackson, Dolly Parton, Charles Barkley, Larry Bird, Diana Ross, The Beach Boys, The Righteous Brothers, Huey Lewis, Liza Minneli, Barbara Mandrel, Larry King, Don 'The Dragon' Wilson, General Swartzkoff and many more.

He has appeared in and served as fight choreographer for action movies as Don (The Dragon's) movie - "Redemption" in the United States and the movie "Shaolin Kid" in Europe. At this time in his life he keeps busy as a corporate Director of Security / Investigations, Personal Protection Specialist, Crises Intervention Instructor, and President of Glenn Wilson's Martial Arts Academies International which are presently located in North America, Central America, Caribbean, Europe and Africa and is absolutely the largest Pai Lum Martial Arts organization in the world! He also serves as Grandmaster and CEO of the largest Pai Lum Tao organization in the world.

Grandmaster Wilson has been training in the martial arts for more than forty eight years. On Glenn's 10th birthday he began what would become a lifelong devotion to martial arts. He started in Kodokan Judo and then moved on to the Kwon styles of Korea. When he was 16 he witnessed a Kenpo demonstration by Master Thomas Dunn that captivated him more than anything he'd ever experienced in the arts. The smooth, fluid and extremely powerful techniques mystified the young martial artist, who to this day holds a major reverence for its curriculum. Glenn studied the various Kenpo disciplines of Tracy's Kenpo, Shorinji Kempo, Kongo Do Kenpo, Chinese Kenpo and the style that would stay with him for life - Bok Leen Pai Kenpo.

He made the natural transition from his Kenpo roots to the various studies of Chuan Fa. Glenn trained in Gong Yuen Chuan Fa, Lo Han Chuan, Moi Fah Chuan, Five Animal methods, White Crane, and Pai Te Lung Chuan of Pai Lum Tao - a style that captured his imagination and gave new meaning to his martial arts pursuits. The internal influences that would help him center his life and training were practiced in Pai Lum Tao's systems of Pai Yung Tai Chi, Quan Nien Chi Kung and Chin Kon Pai Meditation.

Glenn's life would change for the good in the mid seventies when he went

Chapter 1 - Introduction

from the private outdoor (very secluded) training of Master Jim Mcintosh to being accepted as a direct disciple of martial arts legend Great Grandmaster Dr. Daniel Kane Pai. Glenn was brought into the Pai Lum Tao System at the rank he held at the time in the Kou Shu of Taiwan - a third higher level black. This was a very rare happening and reserved for only the few warriors with honor, courage and an very high level of martial skill. Then in 1979 Dr. Pai elevated Glenn to Master and named him head of his family of Pai Lum Tao martial arts. That was ordained the 'Gong Yuen Chuan Fa' family of Pai Lum Tao Martial Arts.

Several years before Dr. Pai's passing he and his disciple, Glenn, formed the White Dragon Warrior Society. The formation was designed to preserve the traditions of Pai Lum Tao, share and strengthen the system and legitimize rank among the families. Dr. Pai served as the Chairman of the Board and Co-Founder, while Glenn was Vice Chairman of the Board of the White Dragon Warrior Society, Inc. (after Dr. Pai's passing Glenn became Chairman of the Board), President of Glenn Wilson's Martial Arts Academies International, and Head Coach of the Wilson's Warriors Competition/ Demonstration Team.

Great Grandmaster Pai died in 1993. This left Grandmaster Glenn C. Wilson in charge of the Society they formed - the White Dragon Warrior Society - as well as Senior Master of his "own" Family of Pai Lum Tao.

Glenn Wilson is considered a grandmaster's grandmaster. He is what a Grandmaster should be: He doesn't talk the game, he lives the life - A Pai Lum Tao Way of Life. I am proud to call him my Pai Lum Brother for more than 35 years. He has been a teacher, brother, and a traditional guru in its highest level.

Master Level – Don 'The Dragon' Wilson

Pai Lum Tao's Modern Lineage

Grandmaster Dr. Seishiro "Henry" Okazaki was a Japanese/ American healer and martial artist. He was born in Kakeda in Fukushima Province, Japan. He emigrated to Hawaii in 1906. He was a very sickly child and through hard training in Kung Fu, Kenpo & Jujitsu, Okazaki recovered completely and vowed to dedicate his life to propagating the Asian martial arts. Grandmaster Okazaki's teachers were Wo Chung – Kung Fu/Chuan Fa and Chinese Kempo, Tanaka Yoshimatsu – Yoshin Ryu, Jujitsu & Judo. These arts as well as the Hawaiian Lua fighting system were the foundation of Grandmaster Okazaki's Danzan Ryu Jujitsu. In addition to the martial disciplines, Okazaki studied health sciences and physical therapy, and ultimately gained a reputation as a healer of the sick and injured. In 1930, Okazaki opened the Nikko Sanatorium of Restoration Massage in Honolulu, which is still in operation today. Many famous personalities of the times came to the Sanatorium to meet, be taught by or be treated by Okazaki. Among the most famous were President Franklin D. Roosevelt, actress Shirley Temple, actor George Burns, and Olympic athlete, actor Johnny Weismuller.

Grandmaster Professor Richard S. Takamoto was the son in law and student of Seishero Okazaki and a well known Hawaiian Kenpo and Hawaiian Lua master teacher in Maui, Hawaii. He operated Kenpo clubs at the Wahiawa YMCA and the Aiea Recreation Center on the Yasuyuki Sakabe Mountain in the late 1940s and the 1950s. Takamoto's reputation as a Kempo/Jujitsu master was widely known and sought after by many martial artists in Hawaii. In 1959 he opened his first school on the mainland USA in Los Angeles, California. Takamoto was one of the earliest and most respected Kenpo teachers in North America.

Grandmaster Dr. Daniel Kalimaahaaee Kane Pai was born in Kameula, Hawaii. Pai is a decedent of Chinese and Hawaiian ancestors. While growing up in Hawaii and having a passion for the Martial Arts, Pai trained with and was influenced by many teachers. Some of them were Wai Tsu Fu Pai, Herman Kane,

Chapter 1 - Introduction

Lum Tai Yung, Henry Seishero Okazaki, Richard Takamoto and his family of Pai, Fong and Po. As a young martial artist he became one of the most prominent fighters of the islands, winning trophies and respect for his family name. In the early 1950s Pai brought his unique system of Pai Lum Tao to the mainland USA. Throughout the mid-sixties and early seventies, he opened schools throughout the United States, with instructors in Florida, Texas, Pennsylvania, Tennessee, Connecticut, Colorado, California, Virginia, Kansas and Canada. During this time he was operating a school in Daytona Beach and had many schools located in Florida. This era peaked with fifty plus Pai Lum and Fire Dragon schools operating in North America. Over the next two decades some of these students, who trained mostly in Kenpo, stayed close to Great Grandmaster - Pai as he trained new students in Kung Fu and Tai Chi disciplines. Pai's reputation grew throughout the world as one of the most feared and respected practitioners of traditional martial arts ever. His effectiveness as a fighter and iron palm master became legendary. Yes, Grandmaster Daniel K. Pai did things his way, and became a true martial arts legend in his own time!

Grandmaster Professor Glenn C. Wilson was born in Florida and began training in the martial arts at the age of ten. Wilson has always had a passion for the martial arts and started in the discipline of Judo. He trained for a very short time in the Kwon styles of Korea then as a young teenager he witnessed the beauty of Kenpo and that became his life long love in the martial arts. It was a natural transition to the art of Kung Fu / Chuan Fa. Wilson is recognized as a true master in both of these arts. Wilson has trained in Kongo Do Kempo, Shorinji Kempo, Tracy Kenpo, Shaolin Chuan Fa, Gong Yuen Chuan Fa, Tai Chi/ Chi Kung and Pai Lum Tao Martial Arts. Together, Wilson and Pai formed the White Dragon Warrior Society to standardize the curriculum, legitimize the ranking and preserve the traditions of Pai Lum Tao. Wilson was named 'Head of his Family' directly by his teacher, Dr. Daniel Kalimaahaaee Kane Pai and he has served this position faithfully ever since. Glenn Wilson has been a world champion competitor, coach and trainer to many world champions, voted into six martial arts hall of fames and continues to be an example of professionalism and guidance to martial artists throughout the world. He continues to travel throughout the world teaching seminars and giving lectures on the traditions of one of the most revered and respected martial arts systems today – Pai Lum Tao.

Chapter 1 - Introduction

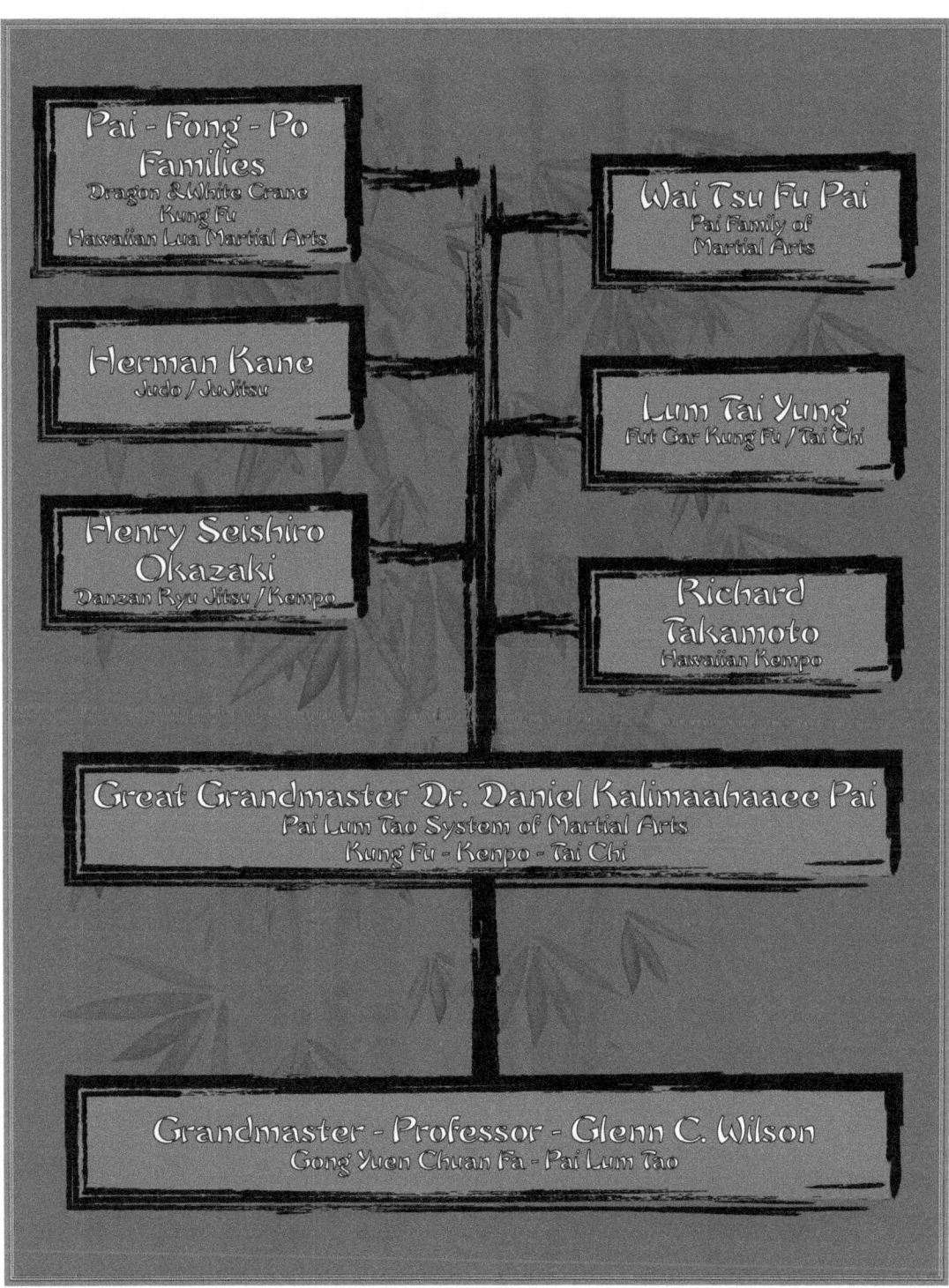

Chapter 2

Philosophy

I Am

I am because of the nights and days I have seen
I believe I am a man for the things I have
done: But all it is, is just feelings of
sensations that are created by my
mind: Those that I touch
know me as I am, these
simple arts that are called
Kung Fu are feelings I
have of the things I now
love: These high sensations
and thrills of my spine,
are not love but a
practitioner's body, that
cares for his art, if I
sound as if I am a
dreamer... Then let me
dream as I practice this
martial art that is called
Kung Fu, These strange
Feelings I have of knowing
The world, Devotion.

By Great Grandmaster Dr. Daniel Kane Pai

Dragon's Code

I am what I am because I choose to Be. I am a Dragon by choice, and Subject to it's laws. My brothers and sisters are my heart and my mind. Even though we may disagree with each other, we still strive to be one. Forgetting all categories and letting energy that wishes to exist, exist. But as a Dragon, I must go forth To seek the Tao and the void, Understanding myself, and finding Peace within.

By Great Grand Master Daniel Kane Pai

The Dragon's Code (Chinese)

白龍道

龍的格言

我就是我,因為這是我的選擇,我選擇做龍,就要遵守這準則,我的弟兄姊妹就是我的心和智。雖然我們間中不妥協,但我們仍然團結一致。忘記你有分歧,而由原動力去生存,去發揚光大。但由於我是龍,我務必要去尋找那道與道之間的真紳,明白自我又尋找我內裡太平,

Philosophical Teachings

Attitude

A proper attitude is essential for proper progress. A person who thinks he knows everything usually knows nothing or just enough to get himself hurt. To study Kung Fu, a student must practice patience, courage, and above all else humility.

A Student must start slowly, and not expect success overnight. If a student goes too hard, too fast, and does not accept the gradual change of body and mind, injury could result. Many injuries result in a student's display of muscle or impatience.

Many new students want to be like a Master, but few have the perseverance to attain such skill. If a student persists in a daily program, lightly at first, he can attain some success in three years, and possibly become a great fighter in five years.

Surely it is worth the effort, for skill brings health, happiness, and confidence. And remember no student can become an expert without first learning how to behave.

The abilities and disciplines to become a master can take 15 to 20 years or a lifetime. But the journey is truly worth the efforts.

The study of Pai Lum Tao is an awakening of the mental, physical and spiritual being. It's teachings focus on a higher level of ones achievement in training. The exercises of Pai Lum Tao have been proven through the experiences of practitioners for the last 1500 years. From the demanding physical training to the levels of meditation attained, it truly becomes an avenue of awareness where one may achieve their goals in life. The 'Tao' of Pai Lum is wisdom, courage, honor, strength, purity and all knowledge.

Students are trained to know themselves. It is believed that this gives purpose to life and ones direction to follow. Once a student has started their journey, they begin to focus positive energy into their training as well as their daily routines. This will open new doors of enlightenment.

The Harmony of Nature

In Meeting which prevails? Ice or Fire? You will probably say fire and you would be correct. However, in dying, does not ice turn to water which will kill fire? This is the harmony of Nature. Each element in turn of importance conquers the other. That prevails which recognizes the power of the other. Conquer your spirit, discipline your mind, train the muscles and limbs to move gracefully. Correct your attitude and be aware of the power of Kung Fu. If you do as I say, you will also prevail.

The Ancient Masters

The ancient masters were subtle, mysterious, silent, profound, and responsive

Watchful, like men crossing a winter stream.

Alert, like men in the jungle.

Courteous, like visiting guests.

Yielding, like melting ice

Simple, like uncarved wood.

Hollow, like caves.

The ancient masters were aware that the flesh dies away and is soon forgotten, but the spirit remains forever.

The Tao

The Tao cannot be defined by words; any words used are one-sided and therefore misleading. Tao is merely a word given to the nameless source of the universe. The universe is the mother of all things, visible and invisible. When you have ceased judging things by yourself, you may see the unseen. Judging things by their relationship to you, you see the visible. But visible and invisible are only words that are different by definition, in essence they are the same. This mystery is a shadow within absolute darkness. Here is the doorway to truth: all things are one! The Tao smoothes the rough surface of life, like gentle rain.

The perfect way (Tao) is without difficulty, it avoids picking and choosing. If you want to get the plain truth, be not concerned with right or wrong. This conflict is a sickness of the mind.

One of the aspects of training developed is called the 'creative mind'. Characteristics of the creative mind are not to be dependent on stimuli with which it comes in contact, nor to be stifled by the reactive mind. It must be active on its own account, functioning spontaneously from the depths of its own nature. Even when initially prompted by something external to itself, it quickly begins to function independently. This aspect of training assures preservation as well as creative growth within a system.

The creative mind can therefore be said to respond rather than to react. Indeed it is capable of transcending conditions altogether. Hence it can be said that whereas the reactive mind is essentially pessimistic (being limited to what is given in immediate experience), the creative mind is profoundly and radically optimistic. By virtue of the very nature of the creative mind, such a reaction would be impossible. On the contrary, the optimism of the creative mind persists despite unpleasant stimuli, despite conditions unfavorable for optimism, or even when there are no conditions for it at all. The creative mind loves when there is no reason to love, is happy when there is no reason for happiness, creates when there is no possibility of creativity, and in this way "builds heaven in spite of hell".

Not being dependent on any object, the creative mind is essentially non-conditioned. It is independent by nature and functions, therefore, in a perfectly spontaneous manner. When functioning on the highest possible level, at its highest pitch of intensity, the creative mind is identical with the unconditioned; that is to say it coincides with the absolute mind. Being non-conditioned or unconditioned, the creative mind is free. Indeed it is freedom itself. It is also original in the true sense of the term, being characterized by ceaseless productivity. This productivity is not necessarily artistic, literary, or musical, even though the painting, the poem, and the symphony are admittedly among its most striking adequate manifestations. Just as the creative mind does not necessarily find expression in 'work of art', likewise, the traditionally called 'works of art' are not necessarily all expressions of the creative mind. Imitative and lacking true originality, some of them are more likely to be mechanical products of the reactive mind.

Outside the sphere of the fine arts, the creative finds expression in productive personal relations, as does our own emotional positiveness. Others become more emotionally positive, or as when through the intensity of their mutual awareness two or more people reach out towards, and together, experience a dimension of being greater and more inclusive than their separate individualities. In similar cases the creative mind is productive in higher states of being and consciousness, contributing to the increase in the world of the sum total of positive emotion. Finally the creative mind is, above all, the aware mind. Being aware, the creative mind is also intensely and radiantly alive. The creative person, as one in whom the creative mind manifests, is not only more aware than the reactive person, but possesses a far greater vitality. This vitality is not just animal high spirits, or emotional exuberance. Where such expressions are permissible, one might say it is the spirit of life itself rising like a fountain from the infinite depths of existence. It flows through the creative person and within all whom one comes into contact.

Pai Lum Tao teaches one to be expressive with their art, to embrace their physical, mental and spiritual sides. A student should understand the art as their 'truth' and it will become their way of life. Of equal importance will be ones virtue. Understanding these virtues will assist daily challenges in their art as well as their lives. They will become more aware of their place in today's social environment. For most of us, the actual self-defense aspect of our training is applied on a minimal basis, where as our social challenges are met and confronted on a daily basis. We will ultimately determine the outcome of these challenges. This, to the Pai Lum Tao practitioner, becomes known as the 'circle of reality'. Understanding and expressing ones wisdom, courage, strength, honesty and love of life will allow the practitioner to tap into their 'inner sources' for help in meeting various challenges.

Much emphasis is put on the theories of mind over matter. To some unexpected trainees it may become mind over matter. There will be some that will prefer mind in favor of matter. Others will denounce mind and uphold the principles of matter. Pai Lum Tao teaches the co-existence of these principals, for mind and matter are inseparable by nature. These particular teachings have truly given support to the practitioner during the rigorous training found within Pai Lum Tao's arsenal of training.

Conflict – whom, when, where, how, what; these encounters are sure to happen to us all. Mastery of the encounter will keep us true to our path. Pai Lum Tao teaches that conflict is OK. What we do with it or about it is what becomes our Tao or Shinto. We are accountable for our actions, whether it be ethically, morally or legally. We will find that so many of our conflicts within ourselves may manifest into resentment, jealousy or fear.

A balanced method or formula of training will help overcome our human behavior that exists at our center. It is important to understand that such behavior must exist, though we do have the means of channeling such emotions. Balanced ideas may stop our emotions from becoming our reality, but we do have a choice. This is evident when we are faced with overwhelming odds, whether they be psychologically or physically. Pai Lum Tao training will surely give the practitioner the clear-cut solution at the moment of reckoning. Some questions the practitioner will ask themselves are Pai Lum Tao's '"Tao of Challenge":

What is the nature of my challenge?

Is it different from my last challenge?

How do I approach my challenge?

How would someone else view my challenge?

How do I feel about this challenge?

What do I know about this challenge?

When do I start doing something to resolve this challenge?

Do I really need to solve this challenge?

Does there really exist a challenge?

Let me now visualize this challenge.

May I seek a wise solution to this disillusion called a challenge?

Expect in the training of Pai Lum Tao to assume states of mind from the very beginning, where in most martial arts, its required only after years of study. The school becomes a new home, fellow students become family members, and the teacher becomes a parent.

Pai Lum Tao teaches one to read before you write, think before you talk, learn before you teach, yield before you fight and know where your thoughts are coming from. The teacher will train the student to walk the way of inner awareness, progress forward in the company of those who practice the way of Pai Lum.

Through our training, we seek the ever-elusive 'enlightenment'. Practicing a balance of physical, mental and spiritual training we surely travel the chosen path. There is no difference between the Zen monk and the martial artist. One is practicing movement passively while the other is practicing stillness actively. Both are on the path to their enlightenment.

Thus Pai Lum Tao asserts that a practitioners material and spiritual needs can be answered through a unified cultivation of training. This realization depends primarily on the individual student's essential habits and insights of their own center. Mastery of ones Pai Lum Tao is no different than the mastery of ones self. The way of life of Pai Lum Tao is a gradual attainment, which finds its answers to all questions within its training. The heart, mind and fist of the Dragon Code of Pai Lum Tao is lived daily by all martial artists. All practitioners must memorize the Dragon Code and be able to recite and explain it on command. This nature of training truly makes Pai Lum Tao a way of life.

Chapter 3

Quan Nien Chi Kung

Chapter 3 - Quan Nien Chi Kung

Basic Concepts

To begin to understand 'basic concepts', you will need a fundamental understanding of some terminology. Quan Nien is the Chinese Goddess of Mercy. Chi Kung literally translates to breath exercise. Chi itself is an abstract term. It is also thought of as the energy that travels through the body. I will delve more into Chi aspects later. Another term that you will need to know is "tan tien". The tan tien is a center point of the body where energy is collected. It is located about one and a half to two inches below the navel.

Some of the benefits of working Quan Nien Chi Kung are stress relief, relaxation of the mind and body, self healing and massaging of the internal organs. The benefit of stress relief is something that is needed in almost everyday life. For some people just driving on the expressway is considered as a high stress experience. Others just need to learn to let the body and mind relax. By letting the body and mind relax it will help the body to recharge and feel refreshed. The massaging of the internal organs in itself sounds a little peculiar. Understanding of the body would let you know that the internal organs, as the body gets older, build up sludge around them and start to solidify. The use of knowing how to breathe properly will help massage the organs and cut down on the sludge build up. It will also increase blood circulation. This will help get the blood flow to all the extremities. Getting fresh blood to the extremities of the body supports overall health and self healing.

Breathing is the most important part of Chi Kung. To help understand the breathing process we must first look at the way a baby breathes. If you watch a baby breathing you will notice that the chest cavity will not expand like an adult's chest does. A baby will use the diaphragm and the belly will rise and fall. Another concept to understand is the amount of air that is pulled into the body this way. Breathing slowly in through the nose, utilizing the tan tien, expanding up to the rib cage, you will have successfully used the diaphragm and been able to take in more air. You are able to pull air in all the way to the bottom of the lungs. Whereas, breathing just from the chest cavity only pulls the air to the center of the lungs. You will exhale slowly out through the mouth. The aspect of filling the tan tien can be compared to blowing up a balloon. The expanding of the balloon all sides are pushed out with the same amount of pressure. As the balloon deflates you will want to have the contraction even on all sides. Utilizing this concept will just imagine a balloon where your tan tien is located.

Another aspect of breathing is that it helps to relax the body. What would happen if the body was to stop breathing? The body would die and then become rigid. The body also becomes rigid from stress and tension. Breathing will help to relax and release the stress and tension. Breathing also determines how the heart will beat, and the heart controls the flow of blood that nourishes and repairs the body.

Movements are another important part. The movements help to move the Chi around the body and also out of the body. One of the main points to remember is not to overextend a movement. Any movement done should not be more than three quarters extension. An example of this would be to extend your arm out to full extension then pull it back about one forth of the way. You should feel that the arm has lost most of the tension that was there just to hold the arm out. That tension that was in the arm is a restrictor of Chi. Energy that is in the body has a difficult time flowing when there is tension.

The movements must also follow along with your breathing patterns. Learning to time your movement and breath together shall take time and patience. The benefits are worth the experience of feeling of relaxation and the flow of Chi. The normal concept is when you strike then you will exhale all of the air that is with in the lungs and as you block you will inhale until the lungs are at complete capacity. This may sound strange that you are striking and blocking, but Quan Nien Chi Kung is a martial art. All of the movements that are taught have self defense applications.

Understand Chi is not something that is easy to explain. Some people might believe that it is a mystical force that only a few or none can obtain. Chi is not anything mystical. Energy is in everyone. It develops differently in every person. Chi is always there. It is just the magnitude in which it is felt that is different. A woman is more susceptible to feeling her own energy before a man. This is the balance between male and female. A male will be physically stronger as a woman would be internally stronger. Chi flows through the body with blood. I had mentioned earlier how breathing controls the heart. So, in essence the breath controls Chi.

My own experience is the only way that I can explain the feelings I have of Chi. The first time that I had ever felt the physical feeling of Chi flowing through my hands was an awakening moment. I was working a basic exercise that is used to help develop Chi. It started out as a little pulsating feeling in my fingertips. I was holding my hands with palms facing each other and then I had the sensation of a physical object in between my hands. The object I felt was a round balloon, which was completely full of air. I was able to feel resistance of the energy on both sides. My hands, after repetitive practice, started to get different responses. They would become very warm and start to feel very heavy. Now, when I am walking down a hallway and I will feel my Chi flowing around me without having to work any of the exercises first.

This is only a basic understanding of Quan Nien Chi Kung. Hopefully, I have given you comprehension of what I have learned. The study of it is something that will take time and dedication. The benefits are worth the time and effort.

Develop Your Internal Power Through Meditation

Meditation is one of the best methods to safely develop your internal power. The purpose of this article is to give you a clear understanding of where your state of mind needs to be as you meditate. Also, it will provide you with the overall understanding of what lies within you for your journey to develop the powerful force within you.

Energy is all around you. The ability to accept it and become acquainted with it is key to meditation. This energy affects the body, mind and spirit. Kirlian photography has been able to show that an energy field surrounds every living thing. There are also some basic drills you can do which will allow you to experience your own energy. One way to do this is to open and close both your hands several times. Then, move the palms of both your hands towards each other (starting from a distance). As your palms get closer to each other you should be able to feel a tingling sensation or even a sense of slight resistance between your palms. The distance between your palms will vary depending on the amount of energy being emitted from your hands. If the energy is strong, you may be able to feel the energy while your hands are 6 inches or more apart. Or, you may need to have your palms nearly touching to feel the sensation. It doesn't matter how far apart your palms are from each other as long as they aren't physically touching each other since that would defeat the purpose of sensing the energy fields between your palms as they intercept. You can also work this with a partner, which will allow you experience the difference between your energy and theirs. Now that you've experienced your own energy, it's of importance to realize that this energy field is affected by our physical and emotional states, so your thoughts, actions and attitudes positively or negatively affect your energy.

Your energy field is made up of chakras. Chakras are recognized across many cultures but are most closely linked to the practice of yoga. A chakra refers to any of the seven energy centers within the body. The chakras correspond to various items, such as color, sound, element, food type, etc. In order to gain a clearer understanding of the chakras within the body (as it applies to developing your internal power), you must have an idea of how they look and where they're located. Imagine a stacked

column of seven "plates" or "wheels of light " within the core (or along the body's spine). In order for you to visualize this in your body, imagine the plate positioned at a corresponding location within the body as follows:

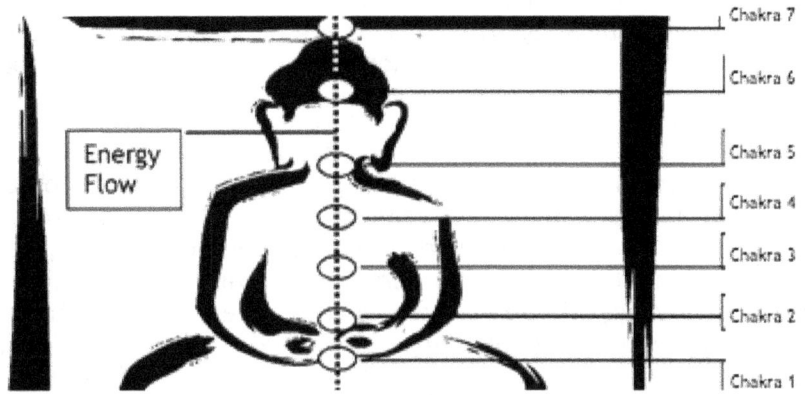

The above picture depicts a model of the chakras along with the energy flowing through the chakras.

Chakra	Location	Sound	Color
Seven	Top of the head	Ng (sing)	Violet
Six	Center of the forehead	Mmmmm	Indigo
Five	Throat	Ee (Sleep)	Blue
Four	Heart	Ay (Play)	Green
Three	Solar Plexus	Ah (Father)	Yellow
Two	Lower Abdomen (Tan Tien)	Oo (Dew)	Orange
One	Base of Spine	"Oh" (Rope)	Red

Now that you have a clearer picture of the chakras as they relate to your own body and energy field, you must also imagine the energy flowing through this column of chakras. Since energy requires both the positive and negative current, each chakra serves as the intersection point of this positive and negative flow of current, resulting in a major energy source corresponding to each chakra location. Visualizing this, you can also think of each chakra as a "battery" located with your body.

The energy within your body is emitted via each chakra as well as the energy, which flows up and down this central column, resulting in the source of your aura or energy field. Although some can see this aura as color(s) or as a vague source of opaque light, the most important point is to understand that you have this tremendous energy system and the capability to nurture it.

The chakras exist in various states such as open, closed, excessive or deficient, yet they are intertwined with each other, which, together, make up your energy system within your body. The chakras are only separated by concept to gain a better understanding of their location and purpose within your body.

Through appropriate meditation techniques, such as sound vibrations or visualization techniques, you have the ability to open all seven of your chakras and unleash the powerful force within you. However, if you expect to put a timetable of a few days or weeks to develop this force within, you would be overly self-confident. The most productive approach is a balanced, gradual effort, like the gentle, continual flow of water. Perseverance and patience are the keys as you enjoy your journey. If you are true to yourself and are able to "tune in" to your own energy, you can develop your own power because it exists in all of us. Our energy system is yet another thing that makes each of use unique like our fingerprints or personalities. Energy systems have distinctive qualities and attributes, no one is better than the other, they are just different.

Once you've developed your internal power, you can harness it with your will or intent to develop the capacity for amazing feats! Although working with your chakras will certainly enhance your martial arts training, whether it's Tai Chi, Kung Fu, Kenpo or SanShou, it also permeates throughout all activities and interactions in your life. Through the knowledge of this system you can positively impact your life in nearly unlimited ways. Some of the ways it can help you are:

Increase power and energy

Increase awareness or receptiveness to compassion

Develop intuition

Increase perception

Combining Pai Lum Tao's meditation tools and techniques along with the knowledge of your energy system, you have the ability to develop your internal power through your positive thoughts, emotions and actions, resulting in a healthy mind, body and spirit.

Quan Nien Chi Kung EE
Goddess of Mercy Breath Excercise One

Start with Pai Yung Tai Chi Salutation.

Body position starts with feet together with inside edge of hand touching thighs.

1. Inhale, lift heels up and angle out to 45 degrees, lift toes up and point forward, lift heels up and angle out 45 degrees again. Knees will be bent in, but not touching. Head level during movement does not rise up.

2. Exhale, tip pelvis forward and align chakras and spine.

3. Inhale, hands rise up in squid fist to about eye level. Elbows must remain at ¾ extension and point down. Pull hands back towards your ears. All done in circular pattern clearing off double lapel grab. Fingers will drag down arms stealing chi. Hands will up at chest level palms forward, fingers pointing up.

Chapter 3 - Quan Nien Chi Kung

4.   Exhale, twin heel palm thrust to chest. Arms do not go past ¾ extensions.

5.   Inhale, fingers will drop down and then point towards other hand in squid fist doing horizontal circles back to your ribs. Elbows remain close to body as squid fist are clearing off a two handed high waist grab. Fingers will drag across arms stealing chi. Hands will end at rib level palms forward fingers pointing out to sides.

6.   Exhale, butterfly palm strike floating rib, arms do not go past ¾ extension. Diaphragm is pushed up with this strike to collapse lungs.

7. Inhale, fingers point in towards each other, hand bent at wrist. Rake down arm with outside blade of hand all the way back to your waist to clear off low two handed waist grab. Technique is called burning the nerves.

8. Exhale, twist hands so fingers point up 45 degree, striking throat with twin spear hands. Fingers must not bend at joints or fingers will bend upon impact.

9. Inhale, finger point down, hands rise up in squid fist to about eye level. Elbows must remain at ¾ extension and point down. Pull hands back towards your ears. All done in circular pattern clearing off double lapel grab. Fingers will drag down arms stealing chi. Hands will up at chest level palms forward, fingers pointing up.

Chapter 3 - Quan Nien Chi Kung   47

10. Exhale, twin heel palm thrust to chest. Arms do not go past ¾ extensions.

11. Inhale, fingers will drop down and then point towards other hand in squid fist doing horizontal circles back to your ribs. Elbows remain close to body as squid fist are clearing off a two handed high waist grab. Fingers will drag across arms stealing chi. Hands will end at rib level palms forward fingers pointing out to sides.

12. Exhale, Butterfly palm strike floating rib, arms do not go past ¾ extension. Diaphragm is pushed up with this strike to collapse lungs.

13. Inhale, Fingers point in towards each other, hand bent at wrist. Rake down arm with outside blade of hand all the way back to your waist to clear off low two handed waist grab. Technique is called burning the nerves.

14. Exhale, twist hands so fingers point up 45 degree, striking throat with twin spear hands. Fingers must not bend at joints or fingers will bend upon impact.

15. Inhale, Fingers point in towards each other, hand bent at wrist. Rake down arm with outside blade of hand all the way back to your waist

Chapter 3 - Quan Nien Chi Kung

16. Exhale, twist hands so fingers point up 45 degree, adjust weight to left leg and adjust left foot to point straight forward pull right foot to left while striking throat with twin spear hands. Hands and feet movement will end at the same time. Body will also rise until there is only a slight bend in the knees.

17. Inhale, turn palms down, hands parallel to floor; hands drop only a little to below chest while going in to a crouching stance.

18. Exhale, pulling hands back into fist in front of body as body rises. Most of the movement of the hands coming back is from the body moving forward on the rise.

19. Inhale, open hands palm up, lifting palms up to chest level while body raises, heels coming slightly off the floor.

20. Exhale, Turn hands over palms face down, hands press down as body lowers with bent knees, ending with fingers pointing down, inside edge of hand against thigh.

If not continuing into Quan Nien Chi Kung Er, then inhale, exhale as body rises. Salutation.

The Chi Kung forms are meant to maximize chi flow trough movement and breathing. Breaths will be done slow and deliberate. Every movement will be matched with maximum inhale or exhale, breathing from the lower tan tien (energy center).

Quan Nien Chi Kung ER
Goddess of Mercy Breath Excercise Two

All the Quan Nien Chi Kung sets should be done in succession. When one ends the next begins. You would not do the salutation in between each set.

Chapter 3 - Quan Nien Chi Kung 51

1. Inhale, shift weight to left leg as right leg becomes light leg, right leg low crescent kick to behind knee, landing in square horse, facing 12:00.

2. Exhale, settling and rooting into square horse.

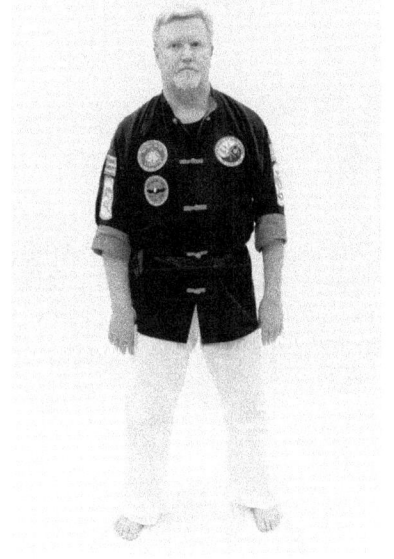

3. Inhale, hands rise up in squid fist to about eye level. Elbows must remain at ¾ extension and point down. Pull hands back towards your ears. All done in circular pattern clearing off double lapel grab. Fingers will drag down arms stealing chi. Hands will up at chest level palms forward, fingers pointing up.

4. Exhale, twin heel palm thrust to chest. Arms do not go past ¾ extensions.

5. Inhale, turning left into seven star stance as palms turn to face inward clearing off with Twin Pines Yuen Chuan and evading left shoulder grab. Facing 9:00.

6. Exhale, pressing forward into shallow long bow striking out with twin heel palm thrust. Alignment of body would be palms over knee, knee over toes, as if your palms, knee and toes would all be touching a wall.

7. Inhale, pulling back into seven star, turn left foot back to 12:00. Body will follow after foot is locked into place. As body turns, palms turn inward clearing off grab to right shoulder with Twin Pines Yuen Chuan.

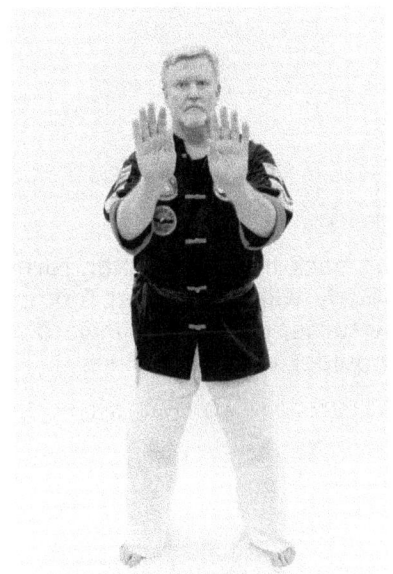

8. Exhale, twin heel palm thrust to chest. Arms do not go past ¾ extensions.

9. Inhale, turning right into seven star stance, as palms turn to face inward clearing off with Twin Pines Yuen Chuan and evading right shoulder grab. Facing 3:00.

10. Exhale, pressing forward into shallow long bow striking out with twin heel palm thrust. Alignment of body would be palms over knee, knee over toes, as if your palms, knee and toes would all be touching a wall.

11. Inhale, pulling back into seven star, turn right foot back to 12:00. Body will follow after foot is locked into place. As body turns, palms turn inward clearing off grab to left shoulder with Twin Pines Yuen Chuan.

12. Exhale, twin heel palm thrust to chest. Arms do not go past ¾ extensions.

Chapter 3 - Quan Nien Chi Kung 55

13. Inhale, turn torso to 9:00 with Twin Pines Yuen Chuan to clear shoulder then with both hands will back hand noni slap and circle down clearing off left should grab. Hands will continue circle to other side of body, when hands pass left knee the knee will follow behind hands as if there was a string attached. Body will turn to 3:00 and then with left leg up turn to 9:00 as palms turn inward and clear with Twin Pines Yuen Chuan. Left leg will be checking opponent's leg.

14. Exhale, left leg will come down with Front Stomp raking down leg then pressing forward into shallow long bow striking out with twin heel palm thrust. Alignment of body would be palms over knee, knee over toes, as if your palms, knee and toes would all be touching a wall.

15. Inhale, turn torso to 12:00 with Twin Pines Yuen Chuan to clear shoulder then with both hands will back hand noni slap and circle down clearing off right should grab. Hands will continue circle to other side of body, when hands pass right knee the knee will follow behind hands as if there was a string attached. Body will turn to 9:00 and then with right leg up turn to 12:00 as palms turn inward and clear with Twin Pines Yuen Chuan. Left leg will be checking opponent's leg. Left leg will still be pointing to 9:00

16. Exhale, turning left foot on heel to 12:00 into a square horse stance. The adjustment will root and propel a waist whip that will be utilized for twin heel palm thrust to chest. Arms do not go past ¾ extensions.

Chapter 3 - Quan Nien Chi Kung

17. Inhale, turn torso to 3:00 with Twin Pines Yuen Chuan to clear shoulder then with both hands will back hand noni slap and circle down clearing off right should grab. Hands will continue circle to other side of body, when hands pass right knee the knee will follow behind hands as if there was a string attached. Body will turn to 9:00 and then with right leg up turn to 3:00 as palms turn inward and clear with Twin Pines Yuen Chuan. Right leg will be checking opponent's leg.

18. Exhale, right leg will come down stomping and raking down leg then pressing forward into shallow long bow striking out with twin heel palm thrust. Alignment of body would be palms over knee, knee over toes, as if your palms, knee and toes would all be touching a wall.

19. Inhale, turn torso to 12:00 with Twin Pines Yuen Chuan to clear shoulder then with both hands will back hand noni slap and circle down clearing off left should grab. Hands will continue circle to other side of body, when hands pass left knee the knee will follow behind hands as if there was a string attached. Body will turn to 3:00 and then with left leg up turn to 12:00 as palms turn inward and clear with Twin Pines Yuen Chuan. Left leg will be checking opponent's leg. Right leg will still be pointing to 3:00

20. Exhale, turning right foot on heel to 12:00 into a square horse stance. The adjustment will root and propel a waist whip that will be utilized for twin heel palm thrust to chest. Arms do not go past ¾ extensions.

21. Inhale, fingers will point down as hand form monkey paws hooking over arms from double lapel grab. Pulling monkey paws back towards your body, just below chest level.

22. Exhale, twin heel palm thrust to chest. Arms do not go past ¾ extensions.

23. Inhale, fingers will point down as hand form monkey paws hooking over arms from double lapel grab. Pulling monkey paws back towards your body, just below chest level.

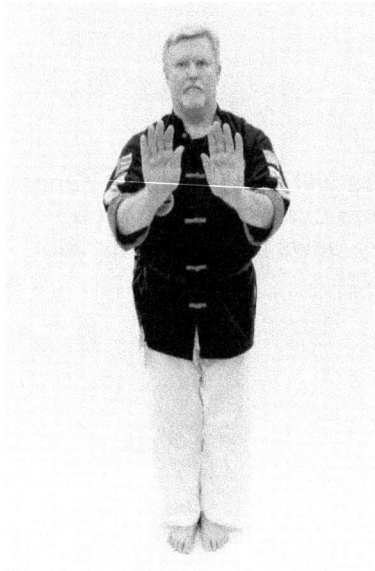

24. Exhale, adjust weight to left leg and bring right foot to left at the same time executing a twin heel palm thrust to chest. Arms do not go past ¾ extensions. Hands will finish strike the same time the right foot settles next to left foot.

25. Inhale, fingers will point down as hand form monkey paws hooking over arms from double lapel grab. Pulling monkey paws back towards your body, just below chest level.

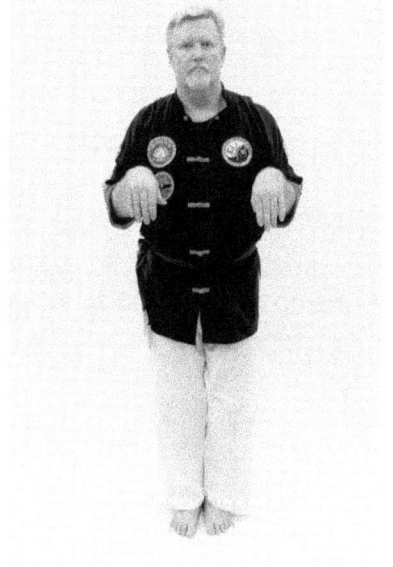

26. Exhale, pressing palms towards the floor ending with fingers pointing towards the floor and inside edge of hand next to thigh. Body will also lower with press.

Quan Nien Chi Kung SAN
Goddess Of Mercy Excercise Three

All the Quan Nien Chi Kung sets should be done in succession. When one ends the next begins. You would not do salutation in between each set.

1. Inhale, shift weight to left leg as right leg becomes light leg, right leg low crescent kick to behind knee, landing in square horse, facing 12:00.

2. Exhale, settling and rooting into square horse.

3. Inhale, hands rise up in squid fist to about eye level. Elbows must remain at ¾ extension and point down. Pull hands back towards your ears. All done in circular pattern clearing off double lapel grab. Fingers will drag down arms stealing chi. Hands will up at chest level palms forward, fingers pointing up.

4. Exhale, twin heel palm thrust to chest. Arms do not go past ¾ extensions.

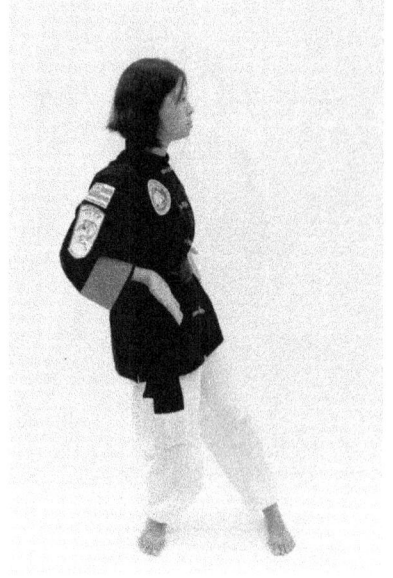

5. Inhale, pull hands back rotating down to chamber palms facing forward and fingers pointing towards the ground as torso turns to 9:00, weight shifts to right leg about 60%, feet do not move. Turn clears off left shoulder grab.

6. Exhale, body presses towards 9:00 shifting weight to left leg 60% with twin heel palm thrust. Hands will go in a straight line from chamber; palms will rotate to point fingers up as strike is in motion.

Chapter 3 - Quan Nien Chi Kung

7.   Inhale, pull hands back rotating down to chamber palms facing forward and fingers pointing towards the ground as torso turns to 3:00, weight shifts to left leg about 60%, feet do not move. Turn clears off right shoulder grab.

8.   Exhale, body presses towards 3:00 shifting weight to right leg 60% with twin heel palm thrust. Hands will go in a straight line from chamber; palms will rotate to point fingers up as strike is in motion.

9.   Inhale, pull hands back rotating down to chamber palms facing forward and fingers pointing towards the ground as torso turns to 12:00, weight shifts to center, feet do not move. Turn clears off left shoulder grab.

10. Exhale, twin heel palm thrust to chest. Arms do not go past ¾ extensions.

11. Inhale, pull back right hand to chamber and torso turns to 9:00 as left hand stay in front and clears with turn, weight shifts to right leg about 60%, feet do not move. Turn clears off left shoulder grab.

12. Exhale, right heel palm thrust as left hand pulls back to chamber, and then left heel palm thrust as right hand pulls back to chamber. Strikes come in on a straight line. Body weight will shift with each strike. (Willow Palm) Heel palm strikes are turned slightly so the position of hand is in between heel palm and willow palm.

13. Inhale, torso turns to 3:00 as left hand stay in front and clears with turn, weight shifts to left leg about 60%, feet do not move. Turn clears off right shoulder grab.

14. Exhale, right heel palm thrust as left hand pulls back to chamber, and then left heel palm thrust as right hand pulls back to chamber. Strikes come in on a straight line. Body weight will shift with each strike. (Willow Palm)

15. Inhale, torso turns to 12:00 as left hand stay in front and clears with turn, weight shifts to center, feet do not move. Turn clears off left shoulder grab.

16. Exhale, right heel palm thrust as left hand pulls back to chamber, and then left heel palm thrust as right hand pulls back to chamber. Strikes come in on a straight line. (Willow Palm)

17. Inhale, left hand turns to left, circles down and pointing palm up as if you were grabbing a wrist and turning it. Pull back to chamber with right leg coming to left leg. Palms up, lifting palms up to chest level while body raises, heels coming slightly off the floor.

18. Exhale, Turn hands over palms face down, hands press down as body lowers with bent knees, ending with fingers pointing down, inside edge of hand against thigh.

Quan Nien Chi Kung SU
Goddess of Mercy Breath Excercise Four

1. Inhale, shift weight to left leg as right leg becomes light leg, right leg low crescent kick to behind knee, landing in square horse, facing 12:00.

2. Exhale, settling and rooting into square horse.

3. Inhale, both arms rise up with crane's heads to clear off double lapel grab as body drops.

Chapter 3 - Quan Nien Chi Kung

4. Exhale, right crane's beak will circle over and hook arm, shifting weight to right leg and turning into seven star stance facing 9:00, right hand in crane's beak continues to 3:00 to throw attacker, left willow palm clears front attacker's arm and strikes in downward circular path to 9:00. The angles of the arms will be 45 degree angle down form right hand to left. Right arm will be even with shoulder and forearm will be 45 degree angle up.

5. Inhale, weight shifts back to square horse facing 12:00 as left wing circles up and right wing circles down to form crane crossing wing guard in front of chest (right in front of left arm), left crane's beak hooks over right arm (hooking over opponent's arm)

6. Exhale, shifting weight to left foot and turning into seven star stance facing 3:00 as left crane's beak clear back to 9:00 throwing opponent, right willow palm strikes 3:00. The angles of the arms will be 45 degree angle down form left hand to right. Left arm will be even with shoulder and forearm will be 45 degree angle up.

7. Inhale, shifting weight back to square horse stance 12:00, torso continues to turn to face 9:00 (arms will be balanced on each side of body when turning), right hand parries at 9:00 and left hand will remain in crane's beak at 6:00, left crane's beak will then circle down, up and open to trap arm pinned between left hand and right shoulder. Right hand forms crane's beak pulling back to right shoulder and hooking over left wrist (hooking over opponent's wrist) torso of body has also turned to 2:00 to help with trap and hook.

8. Exhale, shifting weight to right leg and turning into seven star stance facing 9:00, right hand in crane's beak continues to 3:00 to throw attacker, left willow palm strikes 9:00. The angles of the arms will be 45 degree angle down form right hand to left. Right arm will be even with shoulder and forearm will be 45 degree angle up.

9. Inhale, weight shifts back to square horse facing 12:00 as left wing circles up and right wing circles down to form crane crossing wing guard in front of chest (right in front of left arm), left crane's beak circles under and over right arm to hooks over right arm (hooking over opponent's arm)

10. Exhale, shifting weight to left foot and turning into seven star stance facing 3:00 as left crane's beak clear back to 9:00 throwing opponent, right willow palm strikes 3:00. The angles of the arms will be 45 degree angle down form left hand to right. Left arm will be even with shoulder and forearm will be 45 degree angle up.

11. Inhale, weight shifts back to square horse facing 12:00 and then hands circle down to front (gathering), bringing left foot to right foot as hand come up (fingers pointing to 12:00, palms up) to throat chakra.

12. Exhale, turn palm over, pressing palms down sides of body as body rises, hands will stop in cambered crane's wings (arms slightly out from body, wrist bent 45 degree angle, index finger touching thigh, chest pushed out.)

Quan Nien Chi Kung WU
Goddess of Mercy Excercise Five

1. Inhale, shift weight to left leg as right leg becomes light leg, right leg low crescent kick to behind knee, landing in square horse, facing 12:00.

2. Exhale, settling and rooting into square horse.

3. Inhale, raise arms up on sides of body to over head in to Buddha posture (fingers pointing towards each other palms up over head)

4. Exhale, arms pull down in front of body palms turn downward at third eye chakra, pressing down to waist level fingers still pointing towards each other.

5. Inhale, lift up from wrists into squid fist up to heart chakra.

6. Exhale, press down with palms to waist level fingers pointing 12:00

Chapter 3 - Quan Nien Chi Kung

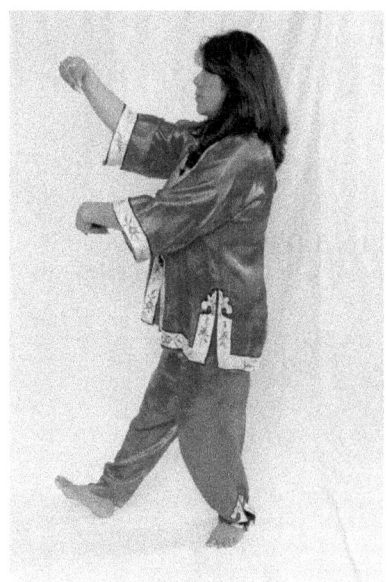

7. Inhale, shift weight to left foot, turning torso to 11:00 while forming loose crane's heads, arms pulling towards 9:00 for waist whip. Turn to 3:00 in seven star stance with right horizontal crane's head clearing to 3:00 and left horizontal crane's head level with right elbow.

8. Exhale, press to 3:00 in long bow striking with horizontal crane's heads.

9. Inhale, shifting weight back to left foot into seven star stance, hands open up and with sticky hands on opponent's arm pull back and down (hands palms down fingers pointing out to 45 degree angles, thumbs pointing down to opposite direction, right hand in front of left. It is not a grab.)

10. Exhale, press to 3:00 in long bow striking with horizontal crane's heads. Right in front of left.

11. Inhale, shift weight back to square horse facing 12:00, arm will pull in front of body in to crane crossing wing guards in front of chest (right in front of left arm) and then press up into Buddha posture (fingers pointing towards each other palms up over head.)

12. Exhale, arms will press out and down from sides of body to shoulder level, arms will rise slightly and then continue to press down (like a slight shudder of wings) all the way down to the side of body.

13. Inhale, pulling fingers inward to point towards each other, palms up rising up to heart chakra.

14. Exhale, turn palms down and press to waist level.

15. Inhale, shift weight to right foot, turning torso to 1:00 while forming loose crane's heads, arms pulling towards 3:00 for waist whip. Turn to 9:00 in seven star stance with left horizontal crane's head clearing to 3:00 and right horizontal crane's head level with right elbow.

16. Exhale, press to 9:00 in long bow striking with horizontal crane's heads.

17. Inhale, shifting weight back to right foot into seven star stance, hands open up and with sticky hands on opponent's arm pull back and down (hands palms down fingers pointing out to 45 degree angles, thumbs pointing down to opposite direction, left hand in front of right. It is not a grab.)

18. Exhale, press to 9:00 in long bow striking with horizontal crane's heads.

Chapter 3 - Quan Nien Chi Kung

19. Inhale, shift weight back to square horse facing 12:00, arm will pull in front of body in to crane crossing wing guards in front of chest (right in front of left arm) and then press up into Buddha posture (fingers pointing towards each other palms up over head.)

20. Exhale, arms will press out and down from sides of body all the way down.

21. Inhale, raise arms up on sides of body to over head in to Buddha posture (fingers pointing towards each other palms up over head)

22. Exhale, arms will press out and down from sides of body all the way down.

23. Inhale, turn hands in palms up and right on top of left lifting up to heart chakra as right foot comes to left foot.

24. Exhale, hands turn over palms facing down left on top of right hand and press down to waist level.

25. Inhale, lift arms up and out to in front of chest level, left on top of right hand arms are rounded.

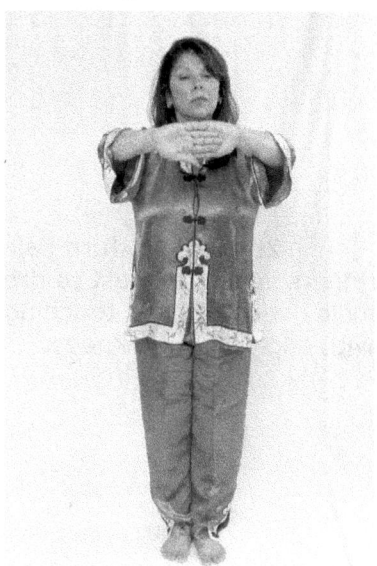

26. Exhale, arms press out to sides clearing when arms are slightly behind twist wrist back and then in pulling to chamber position, palms up.

27. Inhale, pull palms up on sides to heart chakra rising slightly onto ball of foot.

28. Exhale, turn palms down and press down fingers will be the last to drop into position with inside wing of hand touching thigh, body will drop with slight bend in knees.

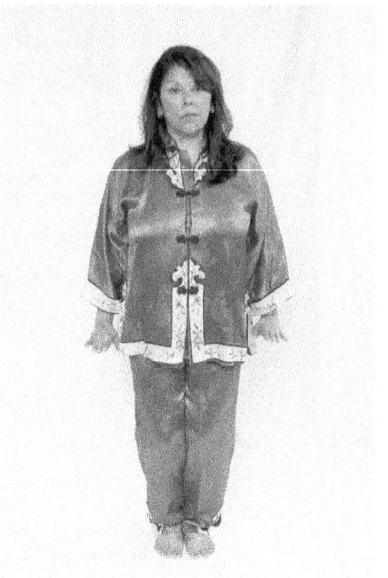

Quan Nien Chi Kung LEIU
Goddess of Mercy Breath Excercise Six

1. Inhale, shift weight to left leg as right leg becomes light leg, right leg low crescent kick to behind knee, landing in square horse, facing 12:00.

2. Exhale, settling and rooting into square horse.

3. Inhale, lift arms up from wrist to heart chakra level.

4. Exhale, press palms down to groin level as body sinks.

5. Inhale, make fist, pull back to chamber palms facing body as body rises slightly.

6. Exhale, punch 45 degree down with both sunfist as body sinks.

7. Inhale, swing arms back behind body as body rises.

8. Exhale, without moving feet adjust into longbow casting right arm out to 10:30 (left arm will be counter balancing right).

9. Inhale, adjust body back to square horse (12:00) as arms come back to hang by sides.

10. Exhale, without moving feet adjust into long bow casting right arm out to 1:30 (right arm will be counter balancing left).

11. Inhale, adjusting back to square horse.

12. Exhale, turn into short bow (9:00) and rise slightly with a right upper gong chuan block and left uppercut. (Arms flow from move 10).

13. Inhale, back to center (body does not come up).

Chapter 3 - Quan Nien Chi Kung

14. Exhale turn into short bow (3:00) rise slightly with a left upper gong chuan block and right uppercut.

15. Inhale, rock back into 7 start stance as left arm comes in front of solar plexus gong chuan palm down., right arm remains in block.

16. Exhale, rolling into long bow while striking with rolling thunder block. (Blocking down with right forearm as left forearm circles over right arm, then blocking down, then right circles over left arm striking down with right back knuckle. Left fist under right elbow).

17. Inhale, turning to 9:00 and rock back into 7 start stance as left arm to block above head (clearing off right arm), right arm comes to solar plexus gong chuan palm down.

18. Exhale, rolling into long bow while striking with rolling thunder block. (Blocking down with left forearm as right forearm circles over left arm, then blocking down, then left circles over right arm striking down with left back knuckle. right fist under left elbow).

19. Inhale, adjust to square horse stance facing 12:00 arms come to crane crossing wings in front of chest (right in front of left arm).

Chapter 3 - Quan Nien Chi Kung 89

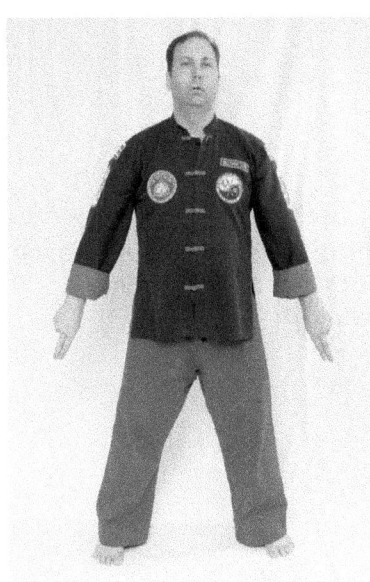

20. Exhale, striking down to both sides with hammer fists, then hands form immortal man points the way (arms do not move while forming immortal man points the way).

21. Inhale, turning to 3:00 into 7 star stance with a blowing windmill block hands remaining in immortal man points the way.

22. Exhale, shifting weight through long bow and ending with left foot behind right knee, while right wrist circles down and left wrist circles over right then right over left (ending with right immortal man in front of left).

23. Inhale, turning to 9:00 into 7 star stance with a blowing windmill block hands remaining in immortal man points the way.

24. Exhale, shifting weight through long bow and ending with right foot behind left knee, while left wrist circles down and right wrist circles over left then left over right (ending with left immortal man in front of right).

25. Inhale, adjusting to square horse (12:00) as arm come to crane crossing wing in front of chest, right in front of left, hand remaining in immortal man.

26. Exhale, arms circle up then out from sides (immortal man stays pointing up).

27. Inhale, left leg steps behind right into monkey as arms continue circle and come up crossed right in front of left.

28. Exhale, right leg steps to square horse when hands separate over head and continue circles. (Important note: The head does not rise up and down with this stepping pattern.)

29. Inhale, left leg steps behind right into monkey as arms continue circle and come up crossed right in front of left.

30. Exhale, right leg steps to square horse when hands separate over head and continue circles to sides.

31. Inhale, left leg steps behind right into monkey as arms continue circle and come up crossed right in front of left.

32. Exhale, right leg steps to square horse when hands separate over head and continue circles to sides.

33. Inhale, remain in square horse as you continue circle in front of body. Hands will come up to level of boxing the face (if you were looking in a mirror hands would look as if they were framing your, arms crossed, palms out facing to sides hands still in immortal man).

34. Exhale, reverse arms to circle down and out to sides.

35. Inhale, as arm cross over head then step with right in front of left into monkey and continue arms circling down.

36. Exhale, as arms separate and come out to sides step into square horse and continue circles up.

37. Inhale, as arm cross over head then step with right in front of left into monkey and continue arms circling down.

38. Exhale, as arms separate and come out to sides step into square horse and continue circles up.

39. Inhale, as arm cross over head then step with right in front of left into monkey and continue arms circling down.

40. Exhale, as arms separate and come out to sides step into square horse and continue circles up.

41. Inhale, staying in square horse arms continue circle out and to the sides of body to shoulder level.

42. Exhale, reverse circle of arms, come down then cross coming up the center line of body as hands fully open up then comes out to sides striking down with arms palms down, wrist relaxed using the weight of the white ape to strike then settle.

43. Inhale, turn to 3:00 in 7 star stance with left inward gong chuan block, right hand chambered.

44. Exhale, rolling into long bow right sunfist to mid zone as left hand comes back past body fist pointing to ground.

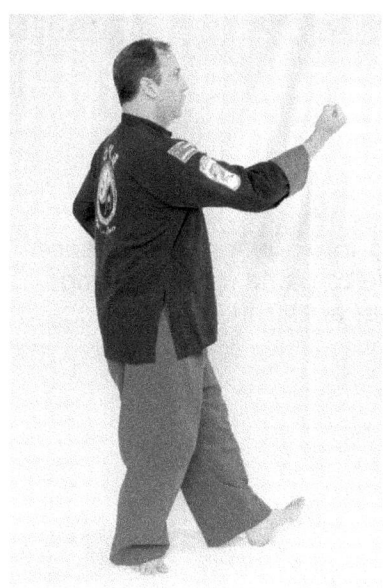

45. Inhale, turn to 9:00 in 7 star stance with right inward gong chuan block, left hand chambered.

46. Regulated exhale, roll into longbow left sunfist to mid zone as right hand comes back past body fist pointing to ground, then step right foot step forward to crouching with right sunfist and left hand chambered, with last part of breath right leg steps back to long bow as left sunfist to mid zone as right hand comes back past body fist pointing to ground.

47. Inhale turning into square horse stance (12:00) while hands come to crane crossing wings gong chuan, bone to bone, at third eye.

48. Exhale, clear down and to sides with gong chuans as body sinks.

49. Inhale, brings hammer fists up to temples (elbow 12:00) as body rises slightly.

50. Exhale, striking down with both hammer fists as body sinks (forearms parallel to floor).

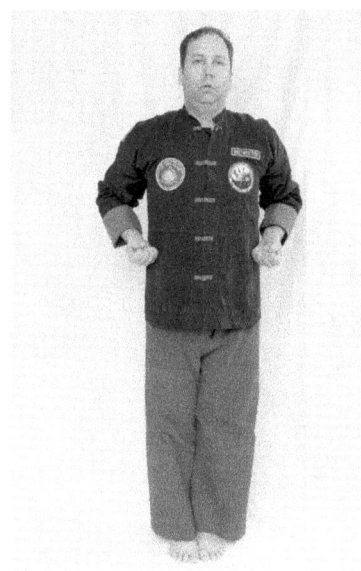

51. Inhale, adjust weight to left foot then bring right foot to left, pulling hands to chamber, rise slightly on ball of feet as pull fist up sides to heart chakra.

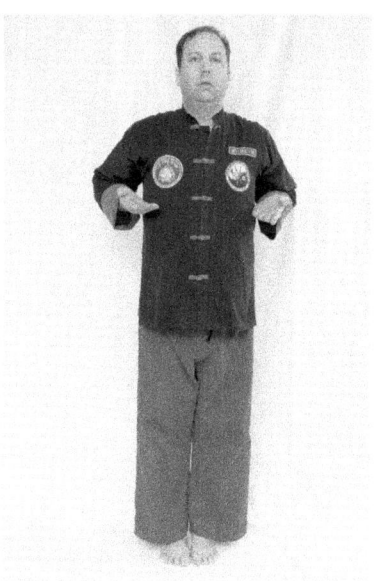

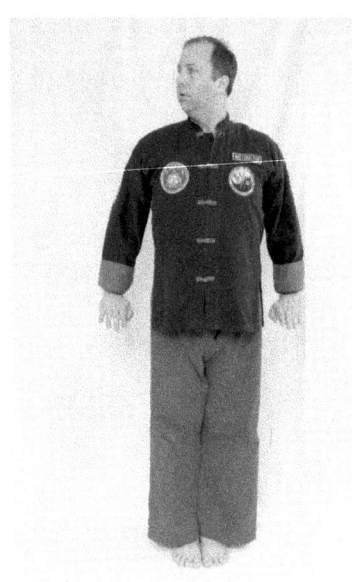

52. Exhale, turn fist over and press fist down side (palm down) while turning head to left.

Chapter 4

Pai Yung Tai Chi

What is Pai Yung Tai Chi Chuan ?

Within the internal Styles of Traditional Chinese martial arts, Tai Chi Chuan is the most popular and widely studied and practiced throughout the world. Within the various styles and systems of Tai Chi Chuan, the Yang style is the most well known to seekers of internal power. It is surley the most popular style found in the world of Chinese Nei Jia Chuan. The basic patterns are both circular and linear fighting moves of modus operandi. Both these theories of motion are combined to produce an ancient fighting structure celebrated as Tai Chi Chuan which literally means the Grand Ultimate Fist.

The continuous practice of Tai Chi Chuans' leisurely, fluid movements will help improve physical stamina by releasing anxiety and stress which causes tension in the body's muscles. It will help prevent bone fatigue while improving ones circulation. One will see great strives in balance and coordination augmented with a significant reduction in their stress levels. The benefits of Tai Chi Chuan have been proven to help diabetes, heart conditions and improve one overall health.

Pai Yung Tai Chi is truly a modern development of an ancient teaching. Dr. Daniel Kane Pai was known for his very rough exterior and knowledge of the most brutal martial arts techniques found on the planet. He became revered and feared as a fighter and a traditionalist in the fighting arts of Asia. Most people did not concentrate on his reverence and passion for the internal arts. He had many secrets to the internal teachings which he shared with only a few students and friends.

The system of Tai Chi Chuan that Dr. Pai taught has become known as 'Pai Yung Tai Chi Chuan.' Pai - honoring is family and the extreme and intertwined knowledge passed down, Yung giving omedge to the 'Old style teachings and applications' of Yang Tai Chi Chuan. The word Chuan is always used when speaking of Tai Chi in the Pai Lum Tao system which translates to, the grand ultimate fist. The chuan must be in the name for everything in the Pai Lum Tao system can be utilized as a supreme self defense or combative art!

The "Grand Ultimate Fist", that truly is Tai Chi Chuan! To uncover the many mysteries of the art will take a lifetime, but the value of the find is unfathomable. What is the 'Pai Yung' system or method of Tai Chi Chuan. Dr. Daniel K. Pai modernized a maturity of internal teachings from his elders and teachers that would rival all systems practiced today! You will find a balance of the 'OLD STYLE' Yang Tai Chi, Wu Style and the treasured Pai family teachings of internal arts within this celebrated Tai Chi style. It is unique and cherished by Pai Lum Tao stylist throughout the world!

To speak of Tai Chi summons a picture of many people, some young, some not so young. All gathered in a park moving together slowly as if doing a dance to an unheard melody. The timing, grace, and peacefulness cast a spell on all who stop to gaze. So many I see drawn to this place to move together in a set pattern. I am compelled to look deeper. I must know this secret, but where to start! I look at the group and observe practitioners of all ages, sizes, men and women moving in harmony and sharing this powerful feeling!

This is a common event in our communities and has become a valued part of our society. The popularity of the Asian arts is ever-growing.

During the 1970s the first form taught to the Tai Chi Chuan students was "Yang Long Form". This long form was taught in several sections and was classic to the preservation of this awesome style. Later in the late 1980s and the early 1990s Dr. Pai worked close with Simo Denise Vigi and Simo Hilda Guerrero Wilson to set a format that would be easily accepted to all students and give them a greater perception of the story being told through the movements of the forms.

Maintaining the 'old style' philosophies and moves of Yang Tai Chi Chuan Dr. Pai set forth that a new Tai Chi Chuan student would learn, 1 – Yang Short Form, 2 – Penetrate the Wind Form then, 3 – Yang Long Form. These forms truly show the serious student the ancient journey between the 'Yang and Wu' philosophies and technical application.

The Pai Yung Tai Chi Chuan forms teach the 'martial' aspects of the internal arts as well as the multitude of health and distressing benefits. So the surprise to many new comers to the internal arts is that Tai Chi really has a history of being primarily a martial / combative art that could be applied with deadly accuracy at any speed, that is the Pai Lum Tao way! Keep in mind that is not to diminish the incredible health benefits of the internal arts, Pai Lum Tao is world renowned for this area of knowledge as well.

The internal arts practitioner will know that the famous Yang Lu - Chan (1799–1872) is considered the founder / father of Yang Style Tai Chi Chuan. The art that he popularized during his life was one of combative implications. There were many secrets found within the 'old style' Yang forms that most schools today do not know and do not teach! It is said that the founder Yang Lu - Chan taught his son Yang Pan - Hou (1837–1890) who had a famous student Wu Chuan – Yu. Eventually Wu Chuan – Yu would teach his own son, Wu Chien – Chuan. During this time of teaching and trading theories the Wu style of tai Chi was born. This blending and forming of philosophies of technique and theory kept the old style combative teachings. Considered by many to be a genius of martial arts, Dr. Pai kept his Tai Chi Chuan true to the old style roots and that is why a modern Tai Chi scholar will see a Yang and Wu marriage of motion!

To date, Dr. Daniel Pai's most proficient student and practitioner of his Pai Yung Tai Chi Chuan was his - love in life, life partner, student and friend, Master / Simo Denise Vigi. Simo Denise Vigi spent the last years of her life teaching Simo Hilda Guerrero Wilson secrets of Pai Yung Tai Chi's movements and applications. Simo Denise would work together with Grandmaster Glenn C. Wilson on their Chi Kung as well as she would get Chi Kung sessions from him up until her passing.

Tai Chi's Mysteries to be uncovered

"The Grand Ultimate", that truly is Tai Chi! To uncover the many mysteries of the art will take a lifetime, but the value of the find is unfathomable.

To speak of Tai Chi summons a picture of many people, some young, some not so young. All gathered in a park moving together slowly as if doing a dance to an unheard melody. The timing, grace, and peacefulness cast a spell on all who stop to gaze. So many I see drawn to this place to move together in a set pattern. Though I do not see anyone leading this movement. No maestro to keep the tempo, but it goes on unwavering as if guided by an unseen hand. What is it this enchantment I see? I am compelled to look deeper. I must know this secret, but where to start! I look at the group and observe. After a while my eyes settle on an elderly gentleman at the far edge of the field by a pond. He is slight of build, frail actually, weathered with a look of the ages. He moves with a particularly fluid grace. I decide; he's the one! I'll ask him what the secret is!

So after he is finished with his movements I politely introduce myself. He responds cordially with broken English. I stumble over the words to use to ask my question because I still do not know exactly what it is I wish to know. Finally, I ask, what are those movements that you were all doing? He looks up at me and tip of his head says, "Tai Chi Chuan!" He sees the bewildered look on my face and directs me to a bench by the shore of the pond. We sit down and he says he will try to explain!

My new friend tells me that it is a centuries old Chinese art form used for health, relaxation, flexibility, meditation and self-defense. The movements help improve balance, and keep the body supple. The concentration and focus that is used helps to quiet the mind and let go of all the needless and possibly damaging thoughts in our life. The best description is that it is a type of moving meditation.

Next I'm told that Tai Chi is change and that the way of nature is to flow freely with it and adapt to any changes. The movements, when practiced correctly, promote the flow of Chi (vital energy) throughout the body. This I'm told is the basis for good or bad health! A good even, unimpaired flow leads to good health. Stagnation or blocked flow leads to illness or poor health.

To help me under stand he showed me some drawings. The first he called the YinYang symbol.

Chapter 4 - Pai Yung Tai Chi   107

I told him that I had seen it before. He smirked and went on to show me another set of symbols.

Supporting Cycle: Sheng

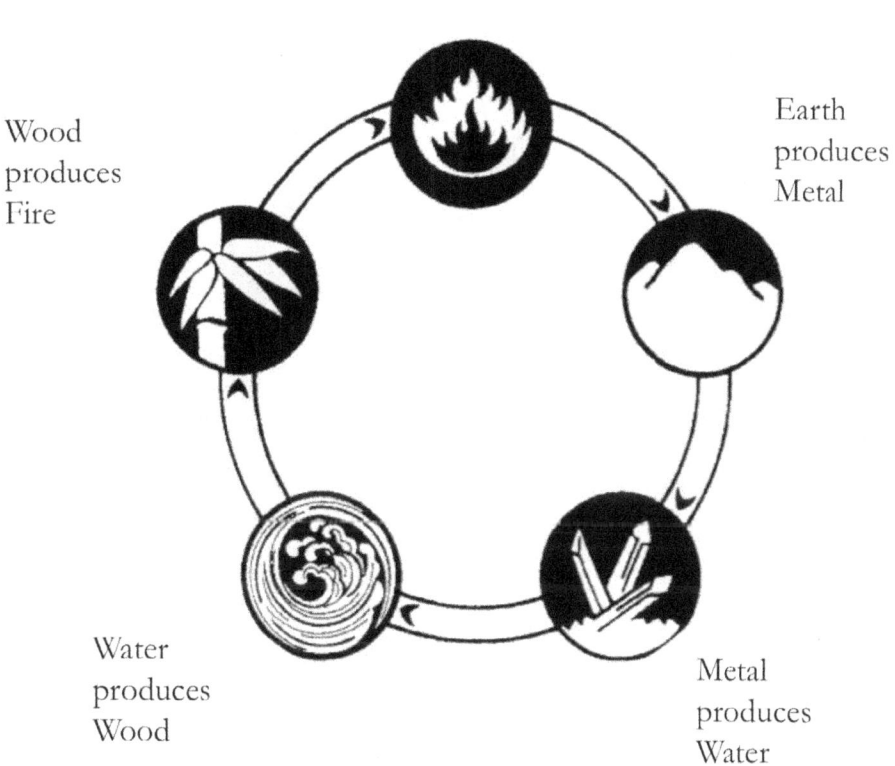

He proceeded to tell me that this cycle is of the "Five Elements" and how they nourish each other in a healthy, normal flow. A stern warning followed! Do not forget Balance! Without a balance of the five elements, nothing good can happen! Of course then I had to ask the obvious question, "How do you keep anyone of them in balance?" Well, now I did it! My friend already knows that my head is spinning, so with a hearty chuckle he shows me a new set of symbols!

Controlling Cycle: Ke

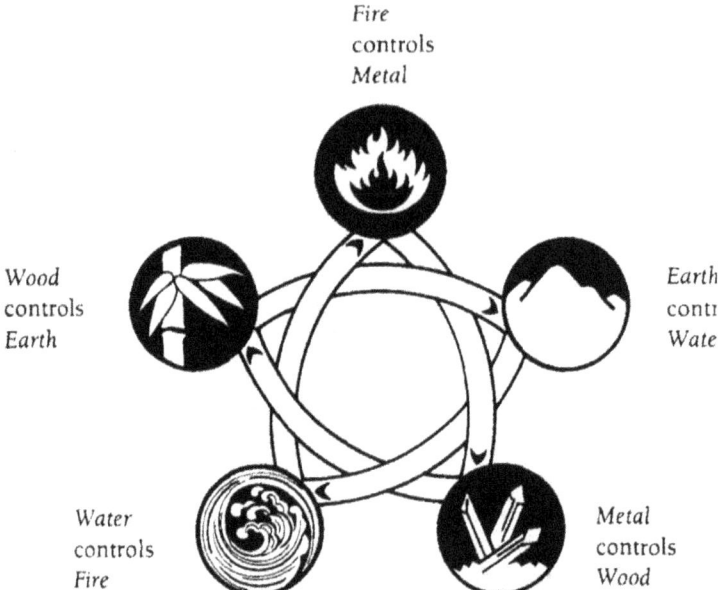

Fire controls Metal

Wood controls Earth

Earth contr Wate

Water controls Fire

Metal controls Wood

This cycle I can understand a little easier. The logic in how they control each other is apparent. I tell him so and he nods. Feeling good now, we continue talking about the balancing act that these elements are playing.

The next thing that I'm told is that these two cycles must come together to form one. He shows me how this is done with another set of symbols.

The Pattern of the Five-Phases

Chapter 4 - Pai Yung Tai Chi

Seeing how the elements work together is one thing, but this doesn't explain to me the affect on a person's health. I mean, I'm not wood, or metal!

I should have known that the answer was their just waiting for me ask! I'm shown how each of the five elements has two sets of organs assigned to it. A Yin set and a Yang set.

	Wood	Fire	Earth	Metal	Water
Yin	Liver	Heart	Spleen	Lungs	Kidney
Yang	Gall Bladder	Small Intestine	Stomach	Large Intestine	Bladder

Using the pattern of the five phases you can map out how either an over abundance or lack of an element can cause an imbalance in our health. Take for example just a simple two - step sequence. If you overindulge in a beverage, let's say coffee, we all know what effect that will have on us. According to the pattern of the five phases too much coffee will insult the large intestine, which will then in turn over produce water. This sounds pretty darn accurate to me!

I see a little about the health side, but how does all this about the five elements come to play in Tai Chi. I know that Chi is the vital energy that nourishes our body by way of the five phases. It's helped to flow by the movements of the body in Tai Chi. Obviously it couldn't be that simple or easy to accomplish since there are so many sick people! If it takes so long to master there must be more to it than just the movements.

So, once again I ask a question I know is going to make my head spin! If the secret isn't the way the elements work together then what is?

It is based in the principle of Yin/Yang. From hard to soft, full and empty, open and close. The five elements however, playa very important part in the Yin and Yang work in harmony with each other. They relate to the five basic stances (foot techniques) in the form; Metal (Advance), Wood (Retreat), Water (Look Left), Fire (Look Right), Earth (Central Equilibrium).

There are also eight hand techniques' which have their foundation in the I Ching or Book of Changes. They are Ward Off, Roll Back, Press, Push, Pull, Split, Elbow, Shoulder.

These together with the five-foot techniques are, "The Thirteen Postures of Tai Chi." They are not to be treated lightly! The thirteen postures are the foundation of Tai Chi and therefore important for students to be trained in them properly.

I tell my new friend that I wish to come back and learn more. He agrees with a smile.

With the day passing, I must bid good day to my new friend. It occurs to me that I never got his name. Sheepishly I ask, "What is your name that I might thank you properly?"

His answer - SIFU

Yang Cheng-fu has said that "the waist is the commander and all movement must go through it." It is also where we generate and store Chi in the Dan Tien. Study every posture. Know its purpose. This is wisdom!

When you practice sink your mind to the Dan Tien and allow the Chi to build and rise up. Keep your spine upright as if suspended by a thread. Stay relaxed and breathe properly down to the Dan Tien. Revel in the feelings. Cherish yourself, you deserve it!

The first step is yours to take. It is important that you understand that it is necessary to have a teacher to help you along this path. The many subtle nuances can be very easily overlooked or misunderstood.

Always remember, "All worthwhile journeys start with a single step!"

Healing Aspects

Chi Kung has many benefits within the use of healing. First you will need to understand more about the physical body and spiritual body. Secondly, a little understanding of how Chi is controlled in the body. Finally, the understanding of how Chi can be used to help others and yourself.

The physical body is in constant use. This use, of course, comes from the daily routines of life. We repeatedly do the same actions every day. We do build up some immunity to doing these tasks, but the body will tire from them over time. This is when we start to get muscle aches. Aches can also be acquired from doing new task, which you have not done before. The body needs to keep itself in balance or else pain will be the outcome.

The spiritual body can also change the way the body reacts. Your thoughts contribute to the way you react to your surroundings. If your thoughts are not in control then you are in danger of creating your own accidents. These can do damage to the physical body. There are many people that consider their selves as clumsy. In reality they are not clumsy, but just preoccupied within their own thoughts. Once you have learned to get clarity to your thoughts and focus upon the moment you are able to have more balance.

Another way the spiritual body controls the body is through stress. The worrying thoughts contribute to different kind of pain within the body. The left side of the body is controlled by female influences and the right side is controlled by male influences. These influences come from either yourself or another person. The understanding of what a person is telling you is important. You are not meant to take on someone else's worries. The same goes for your own worries. The concept of worry is meant as dwelling upon something that cannot be changed or fixed at that moment. You can contemplate a plan to fix the problem, but if nothing comes to mind then you need to get the thoughts out of your head, until a solution can be obtained. Besides being influenced by right or left side, stress will go to different parts of the body. A couple of examples are restricted rotation of the neck means not wanting to look back at past event. The upper portion of the shoulders represents the weight of the world being placed upon you. The upper back stores the stress of someone pushing you to do something. One final example would be the lower back and that signifies worrying about finances. Remember these can be acquired from your own thoughts or others around you.

Understanding Chi flow through the body is something that will take time and practice. Your Chi is moved around through your body by your blood and breath. Just as the heart and lungs depend on each other to work, so does the Chi depend upon the blood and breath. Your body depends upon all three aspects of blood flow, breath (oxygen) and Chi (life force). If you reduce or take away any of these three, then the body will suffer. Your emotions also control the aspect of Chi flow. The best emotions to control Chi flow are love and hate. These emotions are on the opposite spectrum of each other. The one we will focus upon is of course love, since we want to heal the body. The emotion of love also includes love of one's self. This is probably the most important aspect for using Chi to heal. The reasoning of this is if you cannot love yourself, then you are restricting the flow of Chi within yourself and it cannot flow freely through you. The other aspect is the love for the person that you are trying to heal. You will also restrict your Chi flow if your feelings for the other are limited.

The use of Chi to help in the healing process has to start with mutual trust. The person that you are working upon must believe that you are going to help them. Without this belief, then there is the possibility of only limited healing. It also depends upon then person wanting to get rid of their pain. A person may wish to hang on to a pain because it makes them significant. They use it as a topic to talk about. It will make them feel if they let go of the pain then they will not have anything that will make them significant. This is why the spiritual body needs to be kept in balance as well. Any person that wishes to be a good healer must also be a good listener.

The next stage is human touch. The use of touch is amazing. You can change a person's mood just by one touch. Your use of touch must have the intent of healing the other to work. Your thoughts and breath can control the directions of your Chi flow. The use of vibrations is another aspect that will bring Chi to the area that you are working. There are many ways of vibrations. The use of larger oscillations can make the feeling in the body as if they were floating upon the water. Smaller oscillations can penetrate further into the tissue as metal can. Energies can be changed from male to female aspects to help with control of Yin and Yang. Male energy will run hotter and can create the aspects of heat like fire. Female energy will run cooler and create the cooling and healing effects of earth.

When you learn to read and understand the body and the person that you are trying to help then you will be able help that person to heal. This is the last concept you must understand. You are only helping the person to heal themselves. Without this understanding, you will only harm yourself if you cannot help the person.

All of these concepts can be utilized upon yourself to help with your own healing process. You just have to use your own intent and training to increase these benefits.

Penetrate the Wind

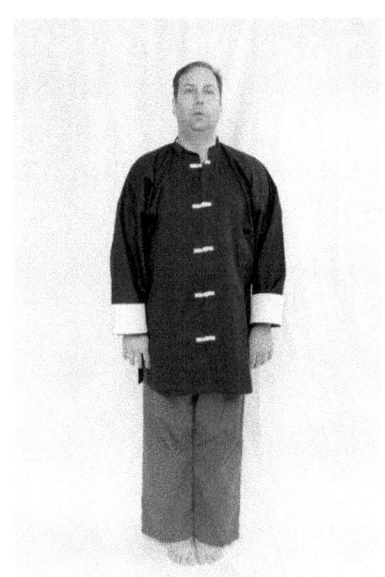

1. Internal Salutation, ending at this position

2. Heel lift and step forward. Yin and Yang

3. Step to left, Yin and Yang

4. Holding the world

5. Penetrate the wind (West)

Chapter 4 - Pai Yung Tai Chi

6. Penetrate the wind (East)

7. Step up and holding the world

8. Monkey paw and inside wing (North)

9. Double gate (West)

10. Front snap kick (East)

11. Penetrate the wind (east)

Chapter 4 - Pai Yung Tai Chi   117

12. Block down (Northeast)

13. Eagle wings (North)

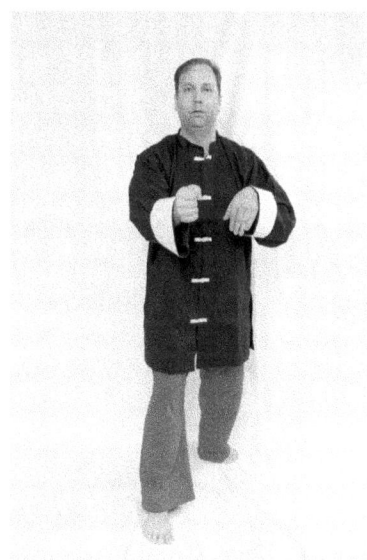

14. Monkey paw, sunfist (North)

15. Double crane's wing inward snap (North)

16. Penetrate the wind (West)

17. Double gate (South)

18. Front snap kick (North)

19. Penetrate the wind (North)

20. Penetrate the wind (South)

21. Crawling snake (South)

22. Penetrate the wind (North)

23. Penetrate the wind (North)

Chapter 4 - Pai Yung Tai Chi

24. Penetrate the wind (North)

25. Embracing the cup (North)

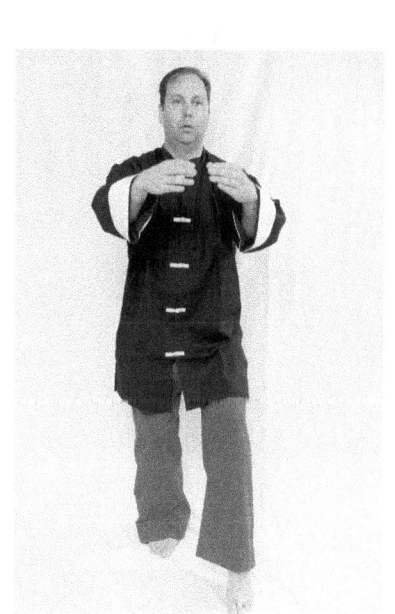

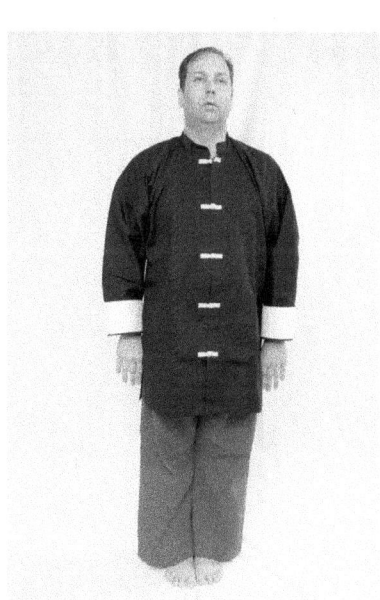

26. Internal Salutation

Yang Short Form

Salutation

Starting Position

1. Heel lift and step

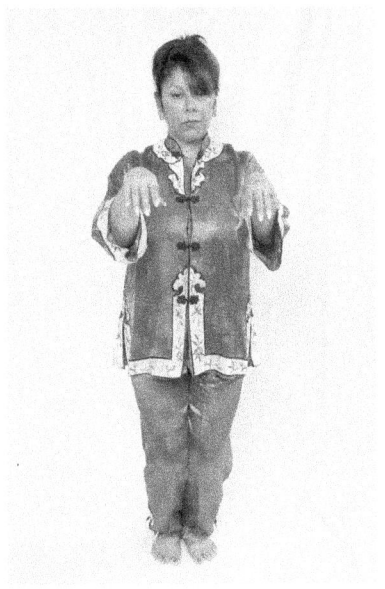

2. Up and down

3. Lean Right

4. Travel left

5. Right hand under chin

6. Fan

7. Little bowl

8. Push little bowl

9. Big bowl

10. Butterfly

11. Push butterfly

12. Brush and strike

13. Chicken

14. Chicken wings

15. Journey to left

16. Slicing to the right

17. Grabbing the thumb
18. Stepping back

19. Double single whip

20. Eagle

21. Body press

22. Pea paw

23. Point
24. Fan

25. Crane cools it's wings

26. Brush

Chapter 4 - Pai Yung Tai Chi

27. Stationary circle

28. Leg lift

29. Pea paw

30. Stationary circle

31. Moveable circle

Chapter 4 - Pai Yung Tai Chi

32. Moveable circle

33. Leg lift

34. Pea paw

35. Stationary circle

36. Fist in open hand

37. Step and chamber

38. Step forward, long bow punch
39. Clear

40. Chicken wings
41. Turn to the right

42. Turn to the front

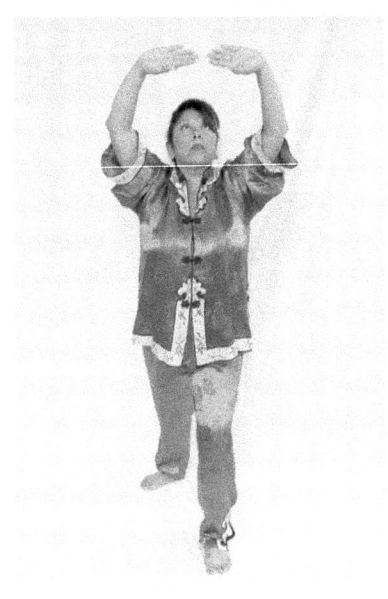

43. Brush the sky

44. Stomp and set

45. Squid fist

Chapter 4 - Pai Yung Tai Chi 137

46. Pressing

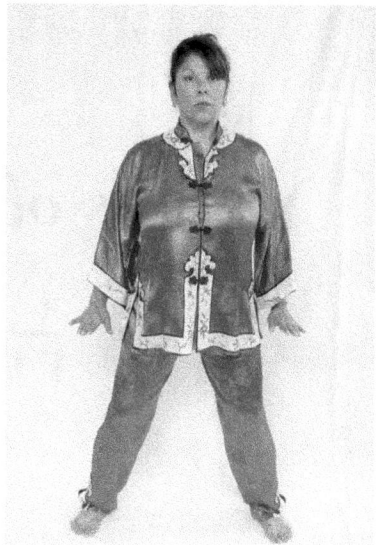

47. Ending position

48. Salutation

Chapter 5

Virtues of the Nine Creatures
and
Five Elements

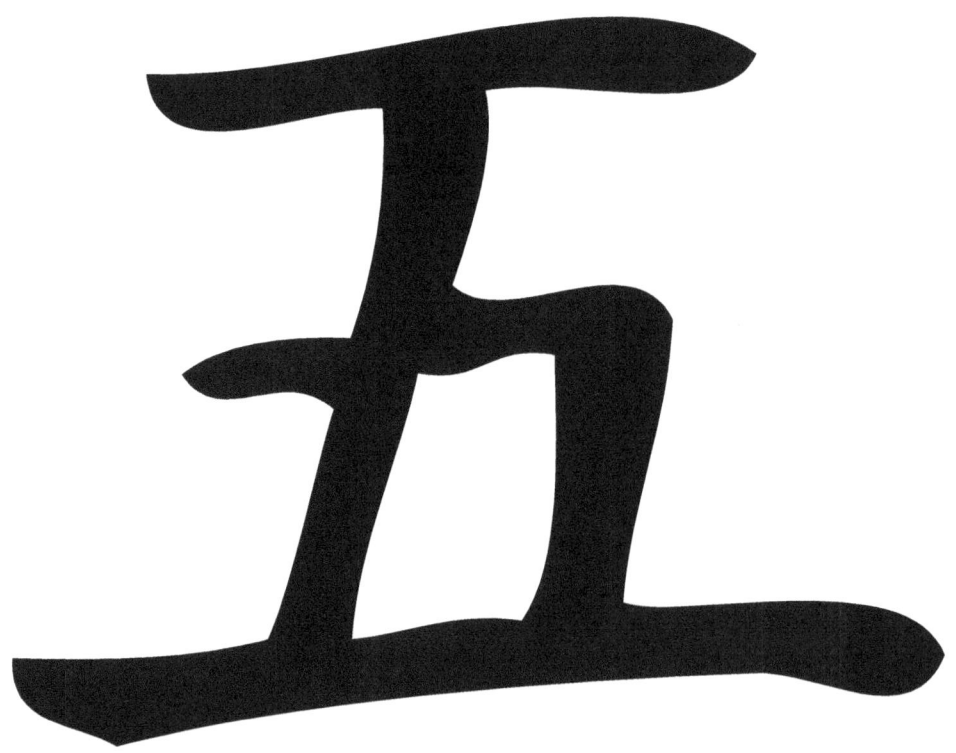

Chapter 5 - Virtues of the Nine Creatures and Five Elements

Pai Lum Tao's Nine Creatures

An intricate part of Pai Lum Tao training is the virtues of the ancient nine creatures. These virtues are practiced diligently by all practitioners as they advance in rank. The virtues will encompass the stances, postures, applications and breathing patterns. These teachings will be found in both the external as well as the internal training divisions.

When practiced in the internal teachings of the Gong Yuen Chuan Fa family the creatures are practiced at a slow rhythmic pace. The eyes are kept closed to enhance ones visualization of the creatures. Then one will practice the intricate breathing patterns, which are unique to each creature. These patterns develop and enhance ones total health.

The Dragon – Spirit

The dragon was symbolic guardian, and was the source of true wisdom. The Chinese dragon, was a long, slender creature, revered as being wise, and was capable of great feats of elusion and power. A dragon could appear and disappear and change form at will. "The Dragon reveals himself only to vanish." Shaolin monks saw him as a vision of enlightened truth, to be felt, but never to be held.

At times the old masters were referred to as dragons, being well versed in the both the healing arts, and kung fu. These skills were a matter of life or death, and those who had mastered them were held in high esteem. They were the masters.

In Pai Lum Tao, the movements based on the dragon incorporate stretching and twisting movements with intricate foot work. Dragon movements often begin with soft circular movements, and end with a hard, sudden explosion of power. Also, the waist is used to generate power in these movements. This demonstrates the whipping action of the dragon's tail.

These movements are used to build the spirit when used in conjunction with proper breathing. The movements should be executed with relaxed, low breathing until the culmination of the strike, at which point, a sudden exhale will assist in the transmission of power.

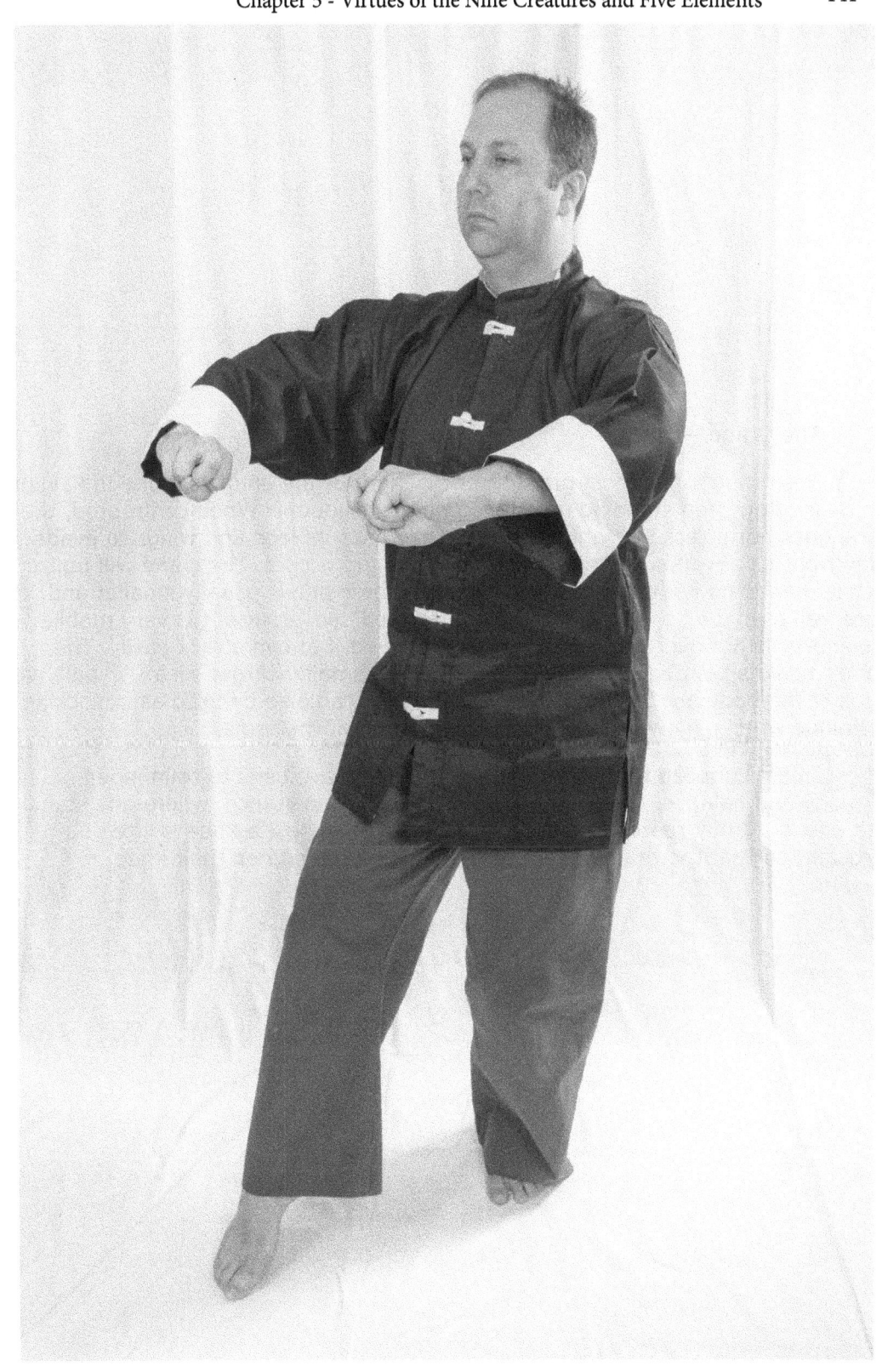

The Crane – Balance

The crane is the most graceful and patient of the animals found in Pai Lum Tao. It is often seen standing on one leg deep in thought. When confronted, the crane does not attack straight on, but instead uses its legs and wings to evade away from its adversary, striking when an opening occurs. The crane will utilize both its beak and its wings to fight. Although the crane is usually smaller and more frail than it's opponent, it can be a ferocious adversary. It is very mobile, this allows it to move where it cannot be attacked, but can attack easily. The crane's beak is pointed, allowing it to strike to a smaller target area, , usually vital areas of the body are targeted. The crane's beak can also be used as a blocking technique when used with a long, circular motion of the arms.

In Pai Lum Tao the movements of the crane are used to train inner harmony and balance. One way to do this is the crane stance, where one stands with one leg firmly rooted into the ground and the opposite knee is lifted up vertically, so that the practitioner could balance a tea cup on their knee.

The Tiger – Bone

In the Pai Lum system we understand that the Tiger fears nothing. It is aggressive and powerful, therefore, when hunting its prey, the tiger does not hesitate in any way. Its strong attacks are so powerful it usually maims or kills in a single blow.

The movements of the tiger are usually straight and incorporate deep, rooted stances from which power is generated. The footwork involved with a tiger movement is firm, and aggressive. The most common weapon of the tiger is the claw. This claw is used to penetrate and tears across a target.

The movements of the tiger are used to develop the strength of the bone, tendons and ligaments. Isometric/tension type exercises are practiced with regulated breathing to assist in ones health.

The Leopard – Muscle

Although a powerful animal, the leopard does not have the size or mass of say, a tiger or ape. Thus, it cannot use just brute strength in a combative situation. Instead, the leopard relies on its efficiency of its muscle and movements coupled with speed. When the leopard pounces on its victim, it will apply a series of fast and unrelenting techniques.

The fast, strikes of the leopard are executed using quick footwork and speedy hands. Because of their quick nature, the movements of the leopard do not emphasize blocking. The leopard would use a slight shift to evade followed immediately by a series of fast attacks. The most common leopard technique is a claw, but unlike the tiger which is both crushing and tearing, the leopard will rake the target.

The movements of the leopard are used to develop muscle efficiency, not the build up of muscle. This develops both power and speed.

Chapter 5 - Virtues of the Nine Creatures and Five Elements

The Snake – Chi

The snake has no legs or arms, requiring it to move using a circular motion of its body. When threatened, the snake is a vicious opponent. The snake strikes with speed and accuracy to vital areas such as pressure points and soft targets. The power of a snake's strike comes from the speed and momentum of its coiled body. It is known for its cunning and soft nature.

To maximize effectiveness, the movements of the snake are executed in long stretched stances, this allows more leverage during striking. The fingertips are used as the main weapon of the snake and are used to penetrate vital areas of the opponent.

Utilizing several breathing exercises coupled with their soft and flowing nature, the movements of the snake are used to develop Chi. These soft, flowing movements will bring the practitioner to a relaxed and peaceful state, allowing them to develop their Chi to a higher level.

Monkey – Cunningness

Within the Pai Lum Tao system Monkey Boxing is considered an elective category of training that few will ever attempt to master. It is considered one of the most physically demanding disciplines which require great flexibility, dexterity and agility. Constantly changing footwork with ascending and descending stances are utilized to confuse the attacker.

The spirit of the monkey must be felt in every move and execution. These exotic moves are matched with a rhythmic breathing that accentuates the technique. The playful attitude of the monkey serves to relax and stimulate the chi flow. With an awesome array of techniques coupled with open chi flow, this aspect of Pai Lum Tao is truly fascinating.

Chapter 5 - Virtues of the Nine Creatures and Five Elements

Mantis – Speed

Utilizing the swift, agile steps of the monkey, the turning evasive body of the Dragon and the lightning hands of the praying mantis, the Pai Lum Tao practitioner enters a deeper understanding of their art. Speed, matched with explosive bursts of air creates an awesome chi exercise that strengthens the lungs. Mantis exercises are patient and waving like the sea, then when the time is right lightening strikes from nowhere.

White Ape – Power

The White Ape is a direct lineage of training in Pai Lum Tao that descends from Tibet. The Tibetan influences in our system include fighting theories as well as Chi development, meditation and herbal training for a total health.

The ape defends quickly using powerful circling blows intended to crush the defenses of it's opponent. The arms are like battering rams that yield to nothing. As the ape swings their powerful arms clearing a path, the body is erect and relaxed. The footwork encompasses long powerful steps and stances that twist and turn. The breathing is long, deep and moves in harmony with the powerful techniques.

Chapter 5 - Virtues of the Nine Creatures and Five Elements

Shark – Focus

The Shark is a direct philosophy and teaching of the Hawaiian Islands. The Pai family clan is the Shark. To our knowledge these teachings are only found in the Pai Lum Tao system of martial arts. The shark practices continuous movement with quick turning body movement and an unwavering focus on their opponent.

The Chi practice of shark is slow and rhythmic in nature. Timing ones airflow with the rotation of the body is key.

Chapter 5 - Virtues of the Nine Creatures and Five Elements

The Five Elements of Wu Hing

Chinese philosophy divides the world into five elements: Wood, Fire, Earth, Metal and Water. These elements are symbolic and represent five forces in nature. The constant interplay between these five forces constitutes the structure and the make-up of creation. All element excercises always begin and end with the White Lotus Posture. The first element is Wood. It represents the life force or spirit, which is responsible for the growth of living organisms in nature (such as trees). This formless life force is usually concealed from our sight by its form, which is Wood, its material structure. Wood burns and gives rise to Fire. From Fire come ashes - Earth. Earth gives rise to Metal (called "Air" in Western occult philosophy). From the Earth with its Metals, Water springs up. Water gives rise to plants and Wood is created. Therefore, Water gives rise to Wood, and the cycle is constantly replenishing and renewing itself. This is creative interplay of the five elements (Sheng cycle). The five elements interplay destructively, meaning they breakdown creation. Disintegration is necessary before regeneration can occur. Therefore, disintegration and generation are but two aspects of the same process (Yin and Yang). The destructive interplay (Ke cycle) is as follows:

Wood destroys Earth - plants break up rocks and soil, ancient wooden plows tilled the soil. Earth destroys Water - Earth absorbs Water,

Earth impedes the natural flow of Water.

Water destroys Fire - Water extinguishes Fire.

Fire destroys Metal- Fire melts Metal.

Metal destroys Wood - Metal cuts Wood.

Lotus

Water

Earth

Wood

Metal

Fire

Chapter 6
Massage

Chapter 6 - Massage

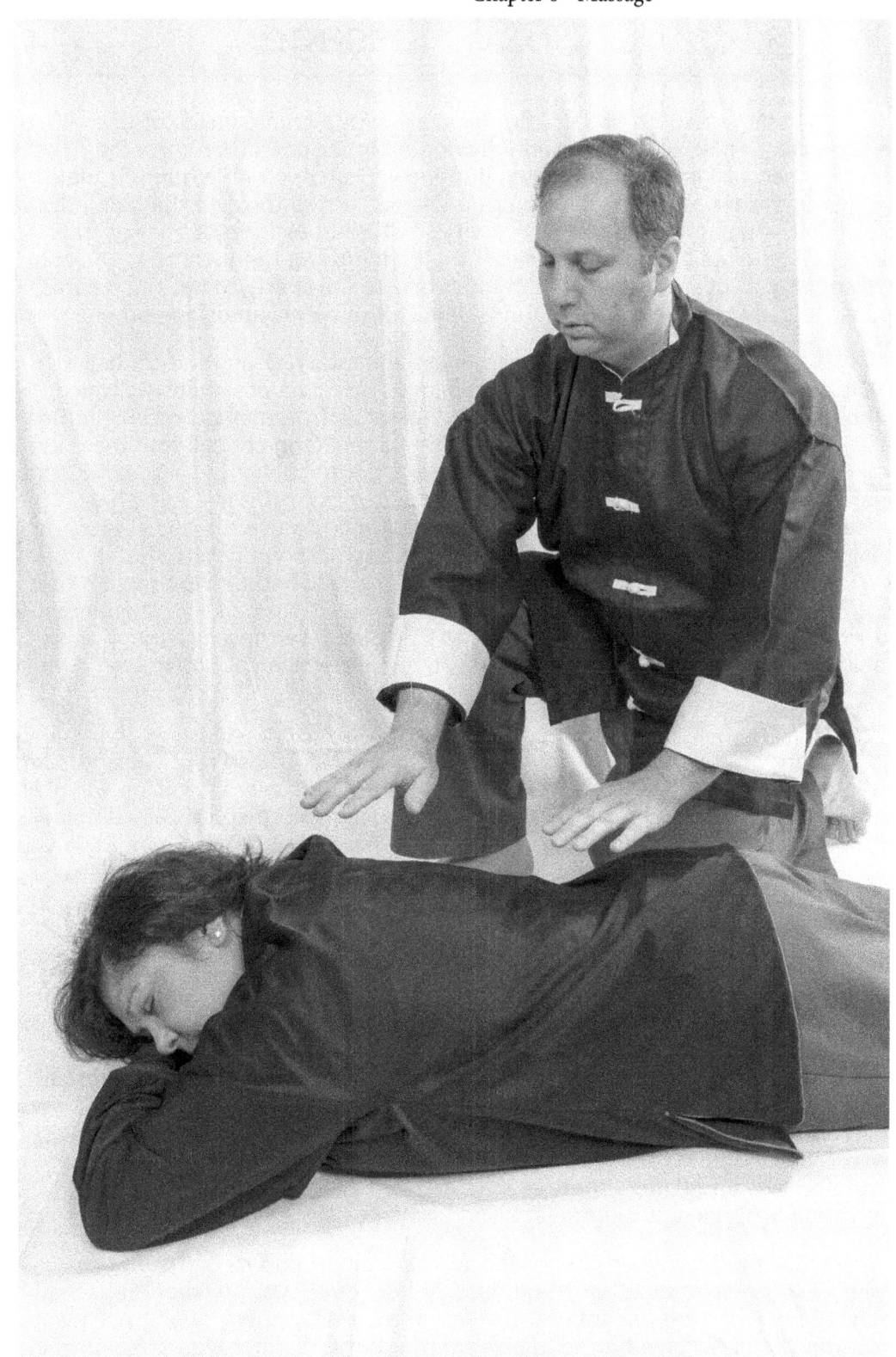

Chi Ball Massage

Chi balls are the metal or ceramic balls with a chime inside of each. There are two balls to a set with one chime having a higher pitch than the other. The higher pitched ball is Yin or female and the lower pitched ball is Yang or male. The chimes create a sound vibration that will be carried through the ball into the person that is being massaged. Vibration is just another form of energy. This energy will be used to access the chi of the body during the massage. The chi balls are only a tool that is used and must be used properly to get the desired results. It is always suggested to get training within a group or one on one.

The chi balls can be used together or separately. Using one chi ball at a time is best when you first start your training. When you are choosing which chi ball to use, Yin or Yang, there are a couple factors. If the person receiving the massage is a woman then you may want to use the Yang chi ball or if male then the Yin chi ball. This is the most basic of choices. The choice can also be changed depending on if it is male or female doing the massage. If it is a male giving the massage and is more Yang nature then he may need to use a Yin chi ball on a female. The same can be said for a female that is more yin nature that is working on a male. Another aspect that will come into play is whether the problem that is being worked on is Yin or Yang deficiency in nature. If Yin deficient then you will use Yin and Yang deficient will use yang. As you can see there are many things you will need to think about just before you choose which chi ball to use.

There are two basic ways of holding the chi ball to use for massage. The first is between the tips of your fingers and thumb. This way of holding will give you the most control over the chi ball. You can use it more specifically and have a little more sensitivity to your touch. The other way is by having it cupped in your palm. The chi ball will be able to roll more, which takes away some of the control. To be comfortable holding and controlling the chi balls will take time and practice.

The chi balls are meant to be used on soft tissue. They can be used on area where there is more bone, but you will need to use very little pressure. The pressure that you will use depends on the individual that is being worked on. There should be a constant communication with this person about the pressure and what they are feeling as you are working. This communication will help you to not hurt the person you are working on as well as let you know if you are helping them. There are times when there may be some discomfort. This discomfort is ok as long as it is not painful. There is a difference between pain and discomfort. The person you are trying to help must also know this before you start.

You should use your other hand to help feel around to find the bony landmarks. The bony landmarks are used to help guide you to where muscles connect to bone. These landmarks are also areas that you will need to be aware of, so you can either avoid or to use very little pressure when you are over the area. Some of the bony landmarks are small and can be easily broken if proper care is not taken.

Using the chi balls you will need to know specific techniques. Some techniques you will be able to do with both of the holding techniques. Practicing with the chi balls will help you to decide what positions of holding will be easier for you. The techniques are pressing, pushing, ironing, rolling and circular

Pressing is done by holding the chi ball in one position and pressing it into the soft tissue. This can be used for areas that have tight muscles or trigger points. When using pressing technique do not press in as hard as you can to start. You should press in gradually and feel for the tissue to release.

Pushing is done by pressing the chi ball in and then pushing it in one direction away from you. This is similar to pressing where you should take care and notice the tissue that you are working on. Some areas will let go faster than others. Do not rush pushing the chi ball.

Ironing technique is done by moving the chi ball back and forth over one area. The pressure will vary according to what is needed. This can be done in short stroke or long strokes.

Rolling technique is done by rolling the chi ball. This can be done with very little pressure. It can be combined with other techniques such as pressing, ironing and circular.

Circular is moving the chi ball in a circular motion. It can be done in small or large circles. If doing large circles then pay attention to where the chi ball is located so you will not use too much pressure in certain areas. Circular can be combined with pressing and rolling techniques.

The chi balls are a wonderful tool to use for massage and with practice and proper guidance you will be able to help out friends and family with different ailments. Get a partner and practice with each other. One of the best ways to understand massage techniques is to have it done to you.

Pressure Points for Health

The purpose of this seminar is to create awareness of the human body and promote a healthy lifestyle. The health and wellbeing of yourself and your loved ones is important. Maintaining it is the hard part.

The points that are being taught will help with certain parts of maintaining this balance of health. A disclaimer needs to be put in at this point. The usage of these points is not meant to substitute for a trained physician. In case of medical situation, the person should be taken to a licensed medical physician.

Intention

The ability to help another person is already ingrained in our makeup. Every person has the ability to help. You can choose to help someone or not. You can even help a person that you do not like. You can also have difficulty helping out a person that you love. The mind is what controls what we are going to be able to do. The mind needs to be controlled to be able to do the most good.

Examples of when the mind is in controlled.

A person that you love is in pain. The first thing that normally happens in the mind is fear. Fear of losing this person.

A person that you do not like is in pain. The mind tells you that you should not care about the person.

These are just basic examples, but it should show the point. Your emotions can control your mind. Emotions and the mind can be controlled by your own thought process. The way to do this is to think of the person as someone that you love. Focus on the task that needs to be done and put love into what you are doing. Love is the key.

Fear is another emotion that will have bad side effects with the mind. Fear has nothing to do with love. Fear is only about you. What you will lose. Fear is a difficult emotion to control. You goal is to focus on what the person needs, not on what your needs are. This is how you will be able to help and not focus on your fear.

Chi (Qi)

Chi is the basis of life. Everything is made up if Chi. Heath is also controlled by Chi. The body has pathways throughout the body that Chi flows through. These are called meridians. Each meridian also has points on the pathway that has access to Chi. When there is disharmony in the body, this means Chi is being impaired. The Chi can be going fast, slow, the wrong direction or just stopped. All of these will impair health in one way or another. By accessing specific points on the body you can help the Chi flow properly through the body.

Vibrational Touch

There are many ways to access the meridians of the body. The one that we will be working with will be with touch, specifically vibrational touch. Touch can be used in many different ways. When someone that you care about is having a bad day and you put your hand on their shoulder, they will normally start to feel better. They can feel the intent that is being sent to them through touch. The opposite can also be shown. If you do not like a person and you put your hand out to stop them from getting next to you, the person will be able to feel it. Vibration is a type of energy and it can quickly access Chi. Like begets like. Through the use of vibrational touch and intent, you will be able to help.

The way to develop vibrational touch is through learning how to oscillate your hand at varying speeds. Start by moving the hand back and forth with larger motions and then make the motion smaller and faster. This does take time and practice. The motion can be done back and forth or up and down. Up and down meaning pressing into the body and then pulling out.

The variation depends on the location as well as the purpose.

When working on a person there is a varying degree of pressure that is used according to the person that is being worked upon. If you are causing pain, then you need to stop. If it is discomfort, then you can continue. Pain is a deterrent. Pain is there to tell you that something is wrong. Pain will cause the body to tense and restrict the flow of Chi and blood. Whereas discomfort is just letting the body know that something happening. When working on a person you need to communicate with them to know that you are not hurting them.

Body measurements

The human body is uniquely individual if you go by the normal measurement standards. If you use the standard measuring units such as inches or centimeters you will not be able to find points on the body. That is why there is a body proportional measurement system. Once you understand these measurements then you will be able to find the points on the body to use.

Cun is the Chinese name that is used for a proportional body inch. It is standard with every person's body and it will change according to the location on the body.

The width of the thumb is 1 Cun.

The width between index and middle fingers is 1.5 Cun.

The width of four fingers together is 3 Cun.

Distance between shoulder blades is six Cun

Distance between nipples is 8 Cun.

Distance between lateral borders of rectus abdominuis muscle is 8 Cun.

Distance between sternocostal angle and umbilicus is 8 Cun.

Distance between Umbilicus and pubic symphysis is 5 Cun.

The use of body measurements is according to the person that is being worked on, not your own. To be able to use your own hand for measurement, you must compare it to the person you are working on.

Points

Stomach 36 (ST-36) Zu San Li- Leg Three Miles- The name Zu San Li is used to help remember that the point is 3 Cun below the knee or that the points helps with three organs; kidney, spleen and stomach. It is also thought as the point to be used if you have walked a lot and need to go another 3 miles.

ST-36 is used to harmonize the stomach, boost and bolster Chi, help nourish blood, clear heat and calm the mind

Location- find the indentation on bottom outside portion of knee cap go 3 cun down and 1 finger's width away from the bone.

Pericardium 6 (P-6) Nei Guan- Inner Pass- The name helps to find the point since it is the inner part of the arm as well as the meridian between the other two yin arm meridians.

P-6 is used to unbind the chest, calm the mind, harmonize stomach to alleviate nausea and vomiting, clears heat.

Location- Find the transverse crease of the inner wrist and go back towards elbow 2 Cun. The point will be located between the two tendons.

Gallbladder 20 (GB-20) Feng Chi- Wind Pool- The name represents a pool in the landscape of the body. Wind is a pathogenic factor that can attack the body. This area is where wind can easily access the body.

GB-20 is used to clear wind, benefits head and eyes, clear the sense organs, and help alleviate pain in neck.

Location- Find the protrusion on skull behind ear and the center/bottom of back of skull. The point is located directly between and is normally tender.

Yin Tang- Hall of Impression- Some associate this with the third eye or the upper Dantian. It is considered as an extra point and not as part of a specific meridian, although it is on the Ren (Conception) meridian.

Yin Tang is used to calm the mind, pacify wind, benefits the nose

Location- between the eyebrows

Spleen 9 (SP-9) Yin Ling Quan- Yin Mound Spring- The landscape of the body, the knee can be thought of as a hill or mound. Since SP-9 is located near the knee and is a water point of the spleen meridian, the name Mound Spring fits. Yin in the name comes from it being on the Yin aspect of the leg (inside portion of leg)

SP-9 is used to help treat energetic aspects of the spleen, resolve dampness, opens and moves water passages, benefits the lower Jiao (lower abdominal organs)

Location- Find the inner (medial) portions of the tibia bone. Follow bone up towards knee until you feel the bone start to curve.

Stomach 44 and Inner Nei Ting- (ST-44, Inner Nei Ting) Inner Courtyard- The name lets you know that it is the space between the toes. Because a courtyard is the space between rooms where there would be quietness from people's voices, this shows one aspect it is used for treatment.

ST-44 and Inner Nei Ting together are used to treat abdominal fullness (bloating) or even some aspects of constipation. ST-44 is used to clear heat from stomach and alleviate pain, harmonize intestines and clears damp-heat, calms mind. Also used for the treatment of aversion to sound of people talking, desire for silence, frequent yawning.

Location- ST-44 is on the top of the foot between the second and third toe and 0.5 Cun back from the web of toes. Inner Nei Ting is directly below ST-44 on the bottom of foot.

Spleen 4 (SP-4) Gong Sun- Grandfather Grandson- The name is also referred as the Yellow Emperor (The Yellow Emperor is a famous Emperor who had the family name of Gong Sun). If Gong is thought of as Grandfather (home meridian) and Sun as Grandson (connecting vessel), this helps to remind you that this point is a connecting point (Luo-Connecting) to the Stomach channel.

SP-4 is used to fortify spleen and harmonize middle Jiao (organs in the middle of the body), regulate Chi and resolve dampness, calm the mind, benefits heart and chest, regulates penetrating meridian (Chong), Good point to use for headaches and menstrual issues.

Location- Find the bone on the inside of foot near ball of foot. Slide finger along bone back towards ankle until it reaches depression at the base of the bone (this is distal and inferior to base of first metatarsal bone)

Kidney 1 (Kid-1) Yong Quan- Gushing Spring- The meaning of the name is that the foot is the lowest part of the body, closest to the earth. A place where water gushes forth from the Earth is a spring. The Kidney channel is of the water element and this point is where energy gushes forth, hence the name Gushing Spring.

Kid-1 is used to descend excess from the head, calm the mind, and rescue

Yang. This is a very strong point and can be very sensitive. The Kidneys are where the essence of the body is stored, which is used to create Chi that is used in the body. When the body gets older the essence is diminished which can cause many problems. One of the main signs of Kidney deficiency would be weak/sore low back and knees. This point can help strengthen the kidneys and in turn help with low back and knees.

Location- Divide the bottom of the foot starting from heel to base of second toe into thirds. Two-thirds from heel and between the second and third metatarsal bones is the location of Kid-1.

These are just some of the points that can be used to help the Chi of the body to move properly. Getting proper Chi flow will encourage a healthy body. Use these points to better yourself and others around you, so we can all have a healthier outlook on life.

Massage

The art of massage is a crucial aspect that every good martial artist should learn. The benefits are the understanding of the human body, better understanding of self and the benefits of balancing the knowledge of hurting and healing.

Understanding of the human body will help you to know how the body moves and how to correct problems. Posture is the first part of movement and can tell you many things if you know where to look. If the posture is off it can help you to control a fight or tell you what muscle is over-contracting and causing disharmony in the body. This disharmony can be causing pain as well as limiting movement.

There is a balancing process that goes on with every muscle. If one muscle contracts then at least one muscle will be stretched, this is the balance. Muscles work against each other. One muscle will contract and move the body and then the other muscle will contract and move the body back. The problem that occurs is when one of the muscles stays contracted. Contracted muscles have an increase amount of blood and stretched muscles have a decrease amount of blood. Over time stretched muscles need more blood flow and pain arises to signal the body. This is the beginning of the pain cycle. Pain is the body requests for more blood to be brought to the stretched muscle. The problem is that the stretched muscle cannot get more blood. A good analogy using a wet cloth is when the cloth is wrung out then the water comes out and when it stays wrung less water will be absorbed. This is one of the keys to understanding the body.

Your understanding of yourself will come about by understanding what your body can do and what you can do to take care of your body. If you are not able to take care of yourself, you will not be able to help others. You need to recognize the disharmonies that happen within your body and get these fixed. The best way is to let someone else help you. Self-treatment is beneficial, but is limited. Allowing someone else to provide care always yields the best results.

The martial artist's knowledge of hurting needs to be balanced with the art of healing. Without this balance the martial artist will only be focused on hurting of others. There is no good that can be gained with only hurting others. The brain and spirit of a person will process this and store it until a later time. This can show up many different ways, such as a mental breakdown or even just pain in the body.

The human body has many moving parts and each is connected to the brain. The brain tells the body how to move and the body tells the brain the sensations that are happening. This process will store information in the body as well as in the brain. A good massage helps to get the pain that is being stored not only in the body, but also in the brain. So, as stated before the knowledge of the human body is important factor to giving a good massage.

Massaging a muscle that is in pain will only help for a short period of time, by moving blood into the area. An example of this is if the upper back area around the edge of the shoulder blades is hurting. The posture that will normally be seen is the shoulders rounded forward. This shows that the chest muscles are contracting and back muscles are being stretched, therefore causing the pain. But, if the opposing muscles in the chest are also massaged then there is less of a chance for the pain to reoccur.

The sense of touch is the best tool used for massage. There are three major sensations that can be felt in a muscle. The first is when the muscle is balanced or in a neutral state. The muscle is relaxed and when you touch it, you will be able to press down to the bone. The second is when the muscle is contracted. The muscle will feel thick and ropy. The third is when the muscle is stretched. The muscle will feel thin and stringy. This is also the area that will be in pain or will feel painful to the person with pressure. The first sensation is what you are working towards with massage. You will want the muscles of the body to be a relaxed state and you will be able to press down to the bone. This may take several treatments to get to this state.

There are many ways to get to this state and you will learn through practice which techniques will help the best. The techniques that will be described are effleurage, petrissage, tapotement, friction and vibration.

Effleurage is a soothing technique that is used to warm up the tissue. It is long strokes skimming on the top layers of the surface. This technique is not deep. This technique is good to start the massage as well as to end. It helps to connect the body to the other parts.

Petrissage is the massage techniques of kneading and squeezing the tissue in a rhythmic fashion. Petrissage will help to move blood in and out of the muscle. It can also be used to make the body to sweat, which is good for a person that has a cold. To help the body to sweat you will squeeze the upper trapezius muscles at a very rapid pace between the fingers and palm of hand.

Tapotament is rhythmic percussion using different parts of the hand, such as finger tips, palm, side of hand and a cupped hand. The rhythmic pounding, tapping or beating is done gently to help the body to relax. The cupped hand is formed by taking the fingers and thumb together and curling the palm in. This will make a raised section in the center of the hand that will not touch when tapping down on person. The cupped area will used the air in the center of palm to send pressure down into the tissue.

Friction is done by use of small movements of the hand back and forth in one area. It is best used with the understanding of the direction of muscle fibers as well as the connection points of the muscle. You will go against the grain of the fibers to create cross-fiber friction. Friction on the attachment of muscles is done to help break up adhesions that are caused from over contractions and small tears formed from building muscle.

Vibration is the movement of going back and forth slowly or very quickly in small or large degrees of movement. The varying degrees of movement will also determine the amount of energy that is released. The most basic is shaking and is considered a large degree of movement and will release the least amount of energy. The small degree will not be seen as much as felt. The practitioners hand will be vibrating very fast, but there will be very small amounts of movement. With this technique you will be able to press into a muscle and feel it start to release slowly and gradually be able to press down to the bone. This technique takes more practice and control from the practitioner.

The use of these techniques can be used individually or combined together, such as using an effleurage stroke and vibration. The combination of different techniques can help to get the body to react faster as well as move energy more effectively. The combining of techniques effectively is more difficult process and it is best to start by mastering individual techniques first. With the mastery of each technique will help you to get mastery of combining.

Massage is a practice that requires love and understanding, time and patience, and hard work. You should practice as much as you can and learn from every person that you will work upon.

Chapter 7

Health and Happiness

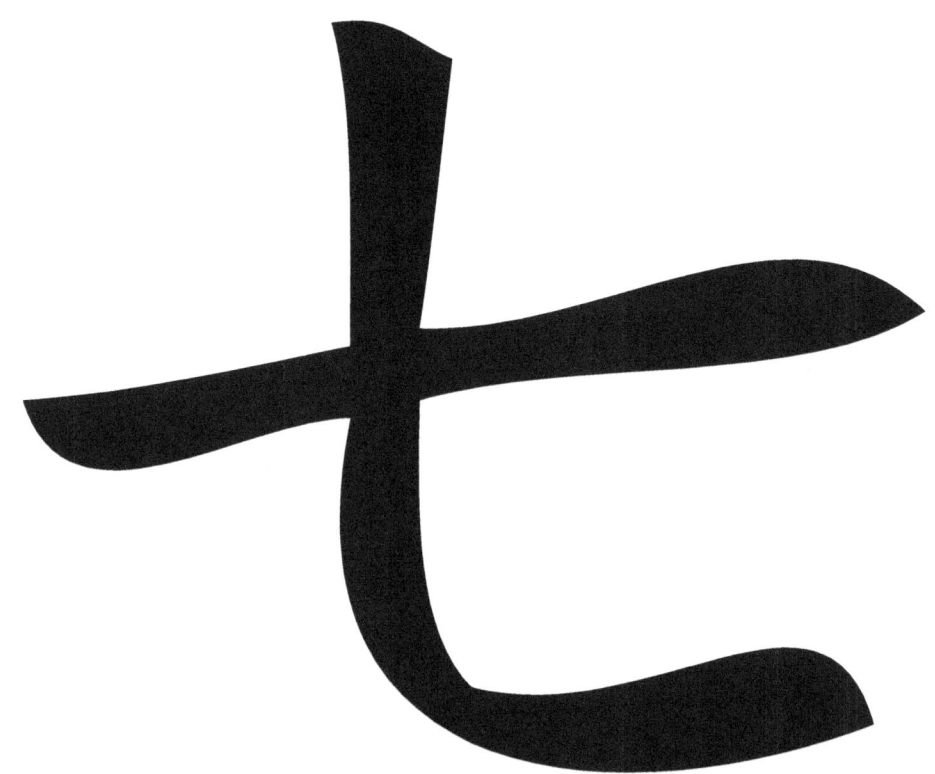

Chapter 7 - Health and Happiness

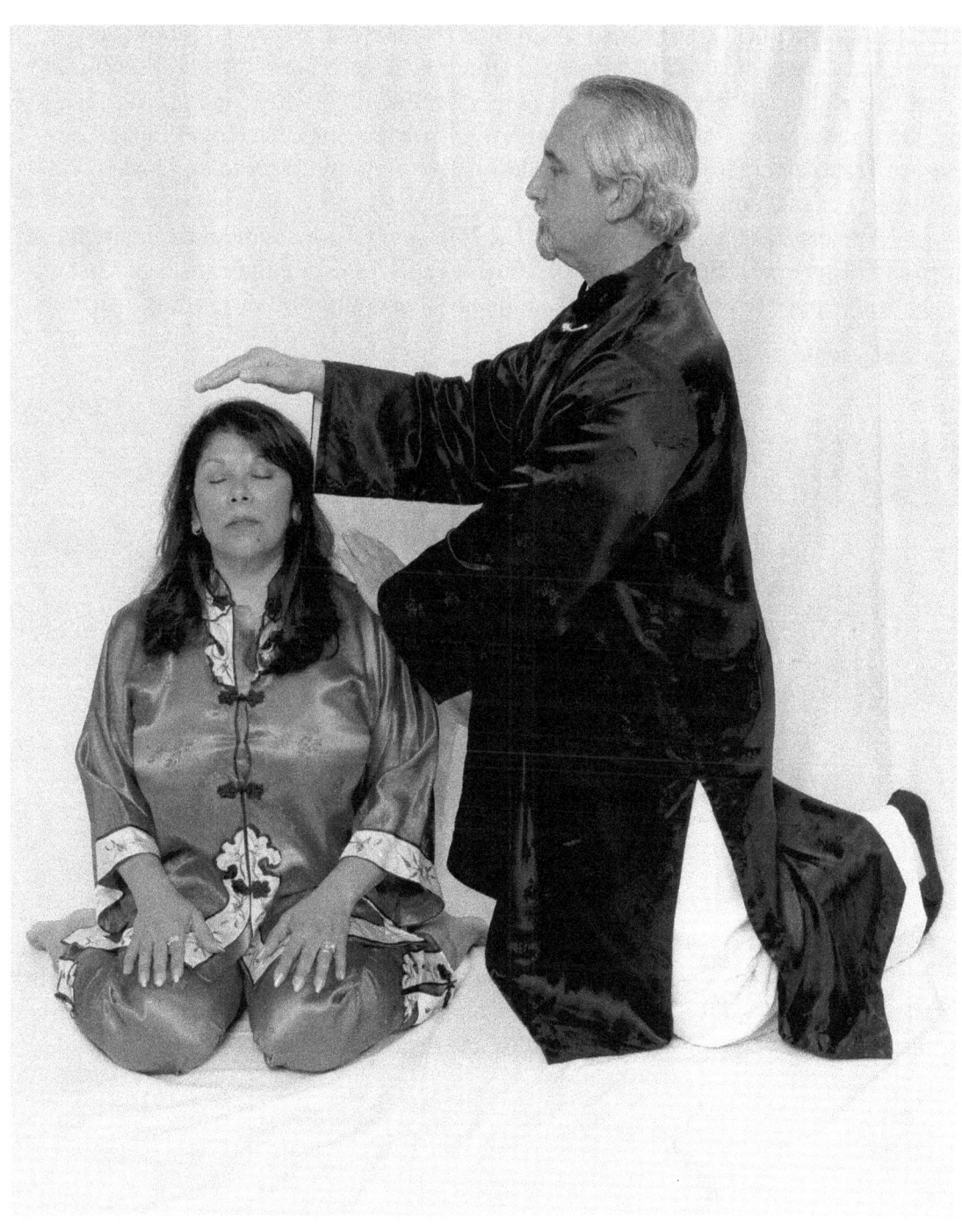

Eight Principles

The "Eight Principles" are the basis of Chinese Medicine. The concept is both very simple and very complex in the same thought. It is based on opposites and combinations. The eight principles are Yin and Yang, cold and hot, interior and exterior, and deficient and excess. They are listed together in their pairings. Each pairing is an opposite of each other. The best way to understand the complexity is to understand the nature of Yin and Yang.

Yin and Yang are put together in the Taiji symbol. This symbol has many meanings and helps to explain the theory of Yin and Yang. There are the aspects of Yin and Yang being opposites, interdependent, mutually consuming and inter-transformation.

Yin and Yang being opposites. This is shows the balance of opposites if there is black then there is white. There are many examples of this in life. The chart below lists some of them.

Yin	Yang
Cold	Hot
Interior	Exterior
Deficiency	Excess
Blood	Qi
Structure	Function
Dark	Light
Death	Birth
Even	Odd
Night	Day
Female	Male
Solid	Hollow
Lower Part	Upper Part
Abdomen	Back
Downward	Upward
Stagnation	Movement

There are many more that can be listed. The few that are listed can help you to understand more of how Yin and Yang can be used to understand more about the body as a whole and this shows the Taiji as a whole with opposite parts.

Yin and Yang are interdependent. Yin and Yang cannot exist without each other. The Taiji has a black section inside of the white and a white section inside of the black or Yin within Yang and Yang within Yin. This shows that you need one to make the other work. You cannot have motion without force. You cannot have matter without energy. They need each other to be able to exist.

Mutual consumption of Yin and Yang is shown when Yin or Yang is out of balance. There is a normal ebb and flow to the balance, but when one becomes too much, it will weaken and consume the other. An example would be when water is evaporated when there is more heat.

Inter-transformation of Yin and Yang is when one will change into the other. When water with heat becomes steam and then when it cools it becomes water again is an example of this.

All of these aspects of Yin and Yang will relate to how the human body will function as a whole. The body is composed of Yin organs and Yang organs. These organs have both a physical function (Yin) and energetic function (Yang). A Yin organ will have both Yin and Yang aspect. This can be broken down over and over. So you can see that it can be very complex or very simple.

Hot and cold is used to determine the objective and subjective temperature of a person. The objective aspect is the actual temperature that is taken of a person as well as touching different areas of the body, such as the feet, hands, abdomen and head, to see if it is cold or hot. The subjective aspect is how the person feels themselves. It is possible for a person to feel hot or cold, but yet the actually body temperature is normal.

Interior and exterior is used to decide if the pathogenic factor is in the interior aspect of the body or exterior. The more interior the pathogen is the worse the problems will be. Interior and exterior can be related to the physical and the energetics of the body. The organs are of course considered as interior and the skin is exterior. There are multiple layers to the skin and then you will have muscles and tendons and bones. There are also different layers of energy channels also called meridians. The meridians relate to the organs as well as different parts of the body. So knowing the different layers of the meridians will help you to know if the problem is more internal or exterior.

Deficient and excess will be used to determine if the body is reacting to the pathogen. The body can be weak causing a deficiency and letting the pathogen into the body. The pathogen itself can also cause the deficiency. An excess can be caused by the pathogen not letting the body to work properly and an excess will build up. This can show up in multiple ways throughout the body.

The use and understanding of how these all combine is just one aspect of learning how to diagnose. There are many others factors that will be needed to help make a proper diagnosis, but these are used to start the path of learning and diagnosis.

We Are What We Eat

In studying the internal arts, one strives to understand the balance of the body. This balance is often represented as the Chinese symbol yin and yang. Over the years, the black and white symbol has appeared in many forms. Yet, yin-yang is more than just a two-dimensional glossy image.

Yin and yang represent opposites in the world. However, there must be caution taken that we don't assign a side as being good or bad. While the Chinese believe in opposites, they don't assign a bad connotation as we would in the Western world. Rather, the two must exist in order for either to continue.

Unlike the flat images, the symbol of yin and yang is in constant motion. In one description, the dark side represents the shadow under the mountain and the light side the sun rising over the edge. As the sun travels across the sky, the dark becomes light and the light dark. The circular motion continues with each side chasing the other.

Tai chi is the application of yin-yang to the body. The movements are circular, generating a flow like the rising and falling of the sun. Energy must come in from outside in order to be sent back out and then brought back in again.

Thus, it is important to understand the forms of energy that come into our body so we can best use that energy within our forms. One of the biggest sources of energy for our bodies is the foods we eat. Food too has a yin-yang aspect to it which must be understood to fully capitalize on its benefits.

The study of food in relation to yin-yang dates back to as early as 2000 BC and documented in The Yellow Emperor's Classic of Internal Medicine, Niejing, the basis for all Chinese medicine. Within this document, the foods are separated into four groups, five tastes, and different classifications.

The four groups are grains, fruits, meats and vegetables. This is similar to the Western concept of food groups. However, the common fifth that is missing in the Chinese classification is dairy/milk. In traditional Chinese cooking, items like cheese and dairy rarely exist. Cow's milk and cheese are items introduced from the West thousands of years after the Niejing was written.

The five tastes are bitter, pungent, salty, sour, and sweet. Five is a very important number in many Chinese concepts and represents a balance much like yin-yang does. When studying the internal arts, you will also come across the 5 elements, which affect the 5 organs of the body, which can each be translated to a particular sound, color, and taste.

The final designation of food into classifications is based on the characteristics of the food. These characteristics can be aligned with being yin, yang or neutral. For instance, many fruits such as apples and watermelons are considered cool and thus follow the "yin" characteristics. Foods such as meats and nuts are "yang" in characteristics.

According to the Niejing, a balanced body will have each of these aspects balanced as well. A balanced meal will contain 3 yang items and 2 yin items, as yin is a much stronger force and does not require the consumption of as much to maintain balance.

It is also believed that if the body is sick or ill the balance within the body, the yin-yang, is lost and can be regained by consuming the appropriate corresponding food. A common example is if you feel a cold coming on, avoid yin foods which will further cool your body and try to increase the yang foods in your diet. If you have a child who is hyper-active, try reducing the amount of yang, energy, in their diet and increasing the yin, calming, foods in their diet. Neutral foods, where the yin-yang is balanced, such as rice, are used to boost the body overall to give it enough energy to perform.

In a perfect world, it would be easy to distinguish the yin, yang, and neutral foods. However, we rarely eat foods by themselves in its pure form. The preparation of the food does not remove the characteristics of the food but rather complicates its nature. So for instance, sweet potato is generally considered a neutral food. However, frying the sweet potato adds the warmer vegetable oil into the mix. The purest form to cook foods is by boiling or steaming, which is why Chinese medicine is normally administered as a boiled tea.

Some examples of foods and their characteristics are:

YIN FOODS	YANG FOODS	NEUTRAL FOODS
Almonds. Apple. Asparagus. Bamboo. Banana. Barley. Bean curd. Bean sprouts. Beer. Broccoli. Cabbage. Celery. Clams. Corn. Corn flour. Crab. Cucumber. Duck. Eels. Fish. Grapes. Honey. Ice creams. Lemons. Mushrooms. Mussels. Oranges. Oysters. Peppermint tea. Pineapple. Salt. Shrimps. Spinach. Strawberries. Soya beans. White sugar. Tomatoes. Water.	Beef. Black pepper. Brown sugar. Butter. Cheese. Chicken liver and fat. Chillies. Chocolate. Coffee. Eggs. Smoked fish. Garlic. Green peppers. Goose. Ham. Kidney beans. Lamb. Leeks. Onions. Peanut butter. Roasted peanuts. Potato. Rabbit. Turkey. Walnuts. Whisky. Wine.	Bread. Carrots. Cauliflower. Cherries. Lean chicken meat. Dates. Milk. Peaches. Peas. Pigeon. Plums. Raisins. Brown rice. Steamed white rice.

The research into Chinese Medicine and the effects of food is still in its infancy and little has been proven in Western terms as to the validity of these methods. Part of the difficulty is that there is no set formula to prescribing Chinese Medicine. Each dose is customized for the individual at that point in time. The same therapy that worked for one person, may not work for another... or even for that same person several weeks down the road. The reason is because Chinese Medicine believes that each person is different and requires different amounts of yin or yang in their body. Over time, our bodies change as well. The most important is listening to our own bodies and finding the balance within.

However, in an article in National Geographic entitled "The Secrets of Long Life" by Dan Buettner, many of the interviewees cite lifestyle and diet have contributed to their ability to live long lives. Balancing the foods you take in will help achieve a healthier you and ultimately bring your energy to your internal arts.

Less Stress = Better Health

Stress attributes to being the biggest killer in our social atmosphere. We are faced with it everyday from the time we wake up until we fight to fall asleep at night. Understanding stress is much more complex than controlling it. We as a society and as individuals must learn to manage, minimize and extinguish it from our lives. So we look at what we can do to be stress less? Relaxation is the tool of choice for most. Now we must understand how do we relax at will or maybe just as often as we are able.

A Swedish physician L. G. Ost developed a progressive exercise for dealing with stress that he called, Applied Relaxation'. These exercises help us deal with confrontations, frustrations, fears and even trouble falling asleep. All of the aforementioned will be directly aligned with stress.

Applied Relaxation has five stages to the exercise!

1. Progressive relaxation
2. Release only relaxation
3. Cue controlled relaxation
4. Differential relaxation
5. Rapid relaxation
6. Applied relaxation

It is common in Pai Lum Tao's internal training to do exercises focusing on these stages. They not only make ones life less stressful and relaxing, they improve the advancement of any martial arts practitioner. An important matter to remember is to adapt ones relaxation techniques to fit your precise need, rather social, private or martial arts. Once a person has learned how to relax at one level, combine different techniques for a more powerful effect.

We all are taught that the different areas of attention are:

1. Thought
2. Breathing
3. Location
4. Comfort

Chapter 8

Blocks

Tai Chi Chuan Blocks

Pai Yung Tai Chi Chuan is known for it's benefits of stress reduction, heightened blood flow, mental clarity and over health benefits. It is also renowned for its self defense aspects effectiveness as is all of the disciplines of traditional Pai Lum Tao training. As in all martial and combative encounters one must successfully deal with the initial assault. The blocks and there applications become very important for the success of the practitioner.

The philosophy of blocking is done with the formula of 'evade and strike'. Unlike many external or 'hard style' martial arts, we do not meet force with force. Tightness and tension are not used to defend against an assault; the movement is smooth, fluid yet powerful.

Blocks are utilized with perfect timing and blending in with the attackers movements. This way the attacker will become off balance and will fall into a vulnerable position. As stated by the ancient master of China: "Control the weight of your opponent and you can defeat anyone."

When defending with Pai Yung Tai Chi Chuan the student will learn to evade and strike with the blending of the attacker's speed, direction and power. Blocking is essential and begins with fluid motion augmented by accelerated Chi flow through the body. The Chi will flow through the defender's body and be expelled into the attacker. With a proper block and deliverance the attacker will be neutralized.

Pai Yung Tai Chi Chuan is very diverse and the blocking patterns encompass Gong Chuan (hard fist), Yuen Chuan (Soft fist) as well as hand postures of the animal and elements practiced within this beautiful art. Grappling and joint lock techniques are common in the arsenal of the mid level and advanced student.

Chapter 8 - Blocks

Double Inward Crane's Wing Snaps

Downward Yuen Chuan

Inward Yuen Chuan

Monkey Paw

Outside Brush

Outward Yuen Chuan

Parting the Clouds

Rake Down

Rising Sun

Squid Fist

Twin Brushing Palms

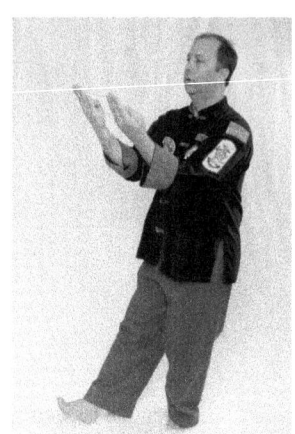
Twin Pines Yuen Chuan

Upward Yuen Chuan

Windmill

Chapter 8 - Blocks

Chapter 9

Punches

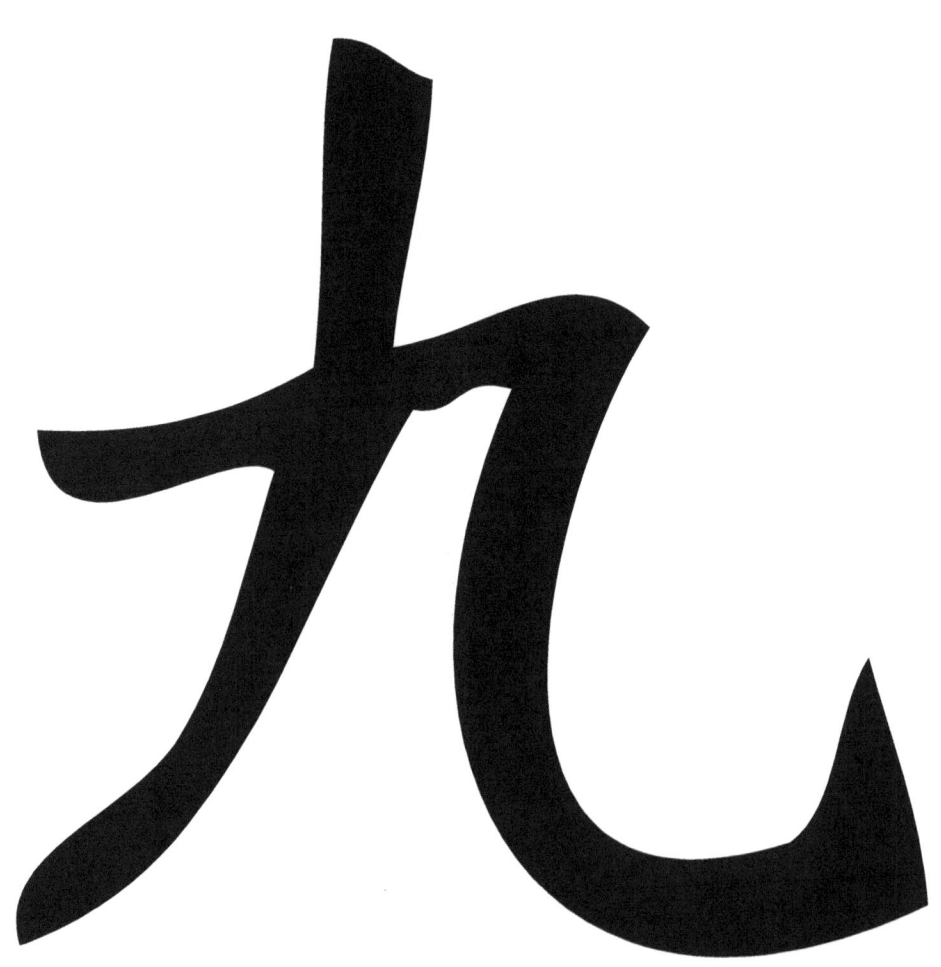

Tai Chi Chuan Punches

The punches found within the internal arts of Pai Lum Tao are as varied and just as important as those in the external arts. The varied categories of hand techniques utilized to strike an attacker are:

- Gong Chuan (hard fist)
- Yuen Chuan (soft Fist)
- Various Animals
- Various elements
- Wing strikes (arms and elbows)

The theory of execution is similar to the external practices within Pai Lum Tao. The total formula and mixing of the essential movements and theories is what differs. The techniques are delivered with smooth, fluid motion that is accelerated with a high level of Chi flow into the attackers vulnerable target area. The hand technique of the practitioner must be relaxed yet precise to its purpose.

All techniques are magnified with the enhanced flow of Chi through ones body. The body will remain relaxed and fluid throughout the movement. This allows Chi to build and explode through the body and out of the arsenal chosen by the practitioner.

When an unsuspecting attacker is hit with the force of Pai Yung Tai Chi Chuan they are startled and amazed at its awesome power and effectiveness. The untrained person has no idea how potent and efficient the combative aspects of Tai Chi Chuan can be. They are distracted with the fluid, beautiful flow of the graceful movements. They do not realize the power within.

The punches and strikes are delivered with a whipping action that magnifies the power and effectiveness at the time of impact. When one thinks of the supple substance of a whip, the leather moves effortless through the air. The winding and flowing motion can be seen as if it is in slow motion then it may explode into a lightening bolt of motion. Upon impact there is a thunderous cracking sound in the air that can be heard by all. The unsuspecting attacker finds themselves on the receiving end of an ancient formula of combative techniques that are extremely beautiful to the eye and rival all with their effectiveness.

Chapter 9 - Punches

Backhand Noni Slap

Butterfly Palms

Crane's Beak

Heel Palm

Immortal Man Points the Way

Inside Crane's Wing

Noni Slap

Outside Crane's Wing

Reverse Inside Crane's Wing

Spear Hand

Sun Fist

Thundering Hammer

White Snake Head

Willow Palm

Chapter 10

Stances

Chapter 10 - Stances

Tai Chi Chuan Stances

In practicing one's art it will always start at the root and then work its way to the rest of the movement. Every traditional martial artist knows that to master your art you must do it in this order:

1. Stance

2. Posture

3. Technique

The stances practiced in Pai Yung Tai Chi Chuan are firm, powerful and solid, yet they are not rigid and stiff. The root and low center of gravity give it the stability needed to create the power and beauty that is so much a part of this ancient art. Do not confuse the fact that the stances are low and solid by thinking that the movements will be stiff or the Chi may be restricted in its flow. That is absolutely untrue.

The stances are divided into two basic categories, stationary and transitionary. The stationary stances are utilized for root development and mustering Chi up from the ground level. This is when the most powerful movements and techniques will be executed. When a practitioner can master their stationary stances, it becomes very hard to move or dislodge them. They are like a power tree that can bend in the wind and not be uprooted.

The transitionary stances are those that are utilized when traveling from one place to another. They are also stances that one will not be in long, just long enough while switching to another stance. Usually blocking and misdirecting strikes are executed from these stances. Rapid fire techniques done to confuse or off set balance are done well from the transitionary stances. Ones center of gravity will be slightly lifted to afford a graceful transition while still allowing techniques to be executed.

Just as in all the disciplines of Pai Lum Tao martial Arts, stances are the first category that the new student will train in. If one does not have good stance, nothing of substance may be built upon it.

Back Stretching Tiger

Buddha Posture

Crane

Forward Pressing Bow

One Legged Monk

Pigeon

Seven Star

Chapter 10 - Stances 203

Dr. Daniel Kalimaahaaee Kane Pai 'Great Grandmaster of Pai Lum Tao Martial Arts' with the love of his life and his leading internal stylist/practitioner for Pai Lum Tao Simo Denise Vigi. May they both rest in peace.

Notes

剛軟拳法白龍道白蓮拳法

Notes

Notes

剛軟拳法白龍道白蓮拳法

Notes

剛軟拳法白龍道白蓮拳法

www.ingramcontent.com/pod-product-compliance
Lightning Source LLC
Chambersburg PA
CBHW080542170426
43195CB00016B/2645